S0-AAD-370

LATIN AMERICA
People and Faith

Sonia Maria Barbosa Dias

United
Methodist
Women
FAITH · HOPE · LOVE IN ACTION

Latin America: People and Faith
Sonia Maria Barbosa Dias
© 2015 United Methodist Women. All rights reserved.

Material from this book not exceeding one-half of published content may be reproduced without adaptation for noncommercial purposes provided the following notice appears with the excerpted material: "From *Latin America: People and Faith* © 2015 United Methodist Women. All rights reserved. Used by permission." Copyrighted material within the book cannot be reproduced without permission from copyright holder.

For all other requests, contact
Director of Mission Education and Enrichment
United Methodist Women
475 Riverside Drive, Room 1504
New York, NY 10115
Fax: (212) 870-3695
Phone: (212) 879-3745

ISBN: 978-1-940182-16-2
Library of Congress Control Number: 2014950629

Cover design: René Ríos
Cover image: Franckreporter/Getty Images
All other photos courtesy of Paul Jeffrey

Printed in the United States of America.

United Methodist Women
PURPOSE

The organized unit of United Methodist Women shall be a community of women whose purpose is to know God and to experience freedom as whole persons through Jesus Christ; to develop a creative, supportive fellowship; and to expand concepts of mission through participation in the global ministries of the church.

The Vision

Turning faith, hope and love into action on behalf of women, children and youth around the world.

Living the Vision

We provide opportunities and resources to grow spiritually, become more deeply rooted in Christ and put faith into action.

We are organized for growth, with flexible structures leading to effective witness and action.

We equip women and girls around the world to be leaders in communities, agencies, workplaces, governments and churches.

We work for justice through compassionate service and advocacy to change unfair policies and systems.

We provide educational experiences that lead to personal change in order to transform the world.

Acknowledgements

I'm thankful to God who created the amazing and blessed chain of events that made it possible for me to know the wonderful work of United Methodist Women which has impressed me by its social and religious commitment, and renewed my faith in God and people.

I would like to express my gratitude to Sara Flores, Ivonne Diaz, Marisa Villareal, Carol Van Gorp, Laurina Gibbs, Kathleen Stone, and my Brazilian sisters Andreia Fernandes, Telma da Silva, Rosângela Oliveira, and Magali do Nascimento Cunha, and all the great women involved in this missionary work. My special thanks to Selby Ewing who invited me to this writing journey and to Praveena Balasundaram for her support and careful attention in dealing with all the demands of the manuscript.

I'm thankful to the group of reviewers: Giseli Gobbo, Luciane Boito, Cadu Matos, Simone Keiko, and the translator, Ariane Correa, who helped me through the labyrinths of languages.

Thanks to Gloriana Tejada who kindly authorized the use of the "Canción por Todos."

To Natalia Noguchi, a great friend, who helped me give life to the book through interviews with people.

Thanks, also, to the people who generously opened their hearts and agreed to share their lives. They made the eight profiles in this book possible.

To my husband, Willem Dias; my boys Pedro and Ulisses; my mother and all my family and friends for their patience and tolerance during my period of writing. I'm thankful for your love and support.

And, to all Latin American people who, with hope and faith, build their history.

Sonia Maria Barbosa Dias

Table of Contents

Foreword

Blueprints are the first detail a builder has to prepare before construction can start. The walls in a building are only a structure until an individual touch is given. For a journalist, writing an article is creating a structure, a house of literature using words to create a unique work.

The information gathering, part of a journalist's job, is not unlike a builder's task as they both put together ideas and thoughts to produce a structure. In Sonia Dias' literary house you can find history, colonization and democracy, art and culture, women in politics, and religion in Latin America. Even though Latin America is a vast area, she offers profiles of people who live in this region, diverse in culture, language, and customs.

As a journalist, Ms. Dias is, foremost, a communicator. She is also a black Latin American woman from Brazil. I am also a black Latin American woman, but born in Panama. We share the main challenges of being born and bred in the region.

The issue of inequality in education where a better education results in best jobs brings about the difference in social classes. The profiles express this well. The profiles are hopeful and encouraging. They focus on the importance of attaining education at all levels and subsequently a better lifestyle.

Four characteristics make this book a must-read:

It is personal. Sonia Dias shares her personal experiences of growing up in Brazil, as a wife, then becoming a professional mother.

It is theological. Even though it is not an expanded Bible study, she expresses God's presence in her writing.

It is informative. It is based on her extensive research and includes short, vivid biographies.

It is inspirational. It will inspire women and men because it drives us to continue moving on and be examples for newer generations.

This study will be helpful to learn about Latin America, its people, and faith.

Carla E. Boyce-Smith
World Secretary of the World Federation Methodist and Uniting Church Women (WFM&UCW)
Iglesia Evangélica Metodista de Panamá
Republic of Panamá

A Wichí indigenous girl in an indigenous neighborhood of Embarcación, Argentina. The Wichí in this area, largely traditional hunters and gatherers, have struggled for decades to recover land that has been systematically stolen from them by cattle raisers and large agricultural plantations. *(Paul Jeffrey)*

Introduction

During a long period of drought in northeast Brazil in the 1940s, my grandfather, his wife, and children left his small farm and crops in Bahia and came to São Paulo to work the coffee crops. After several years, he was able to buy a house and work as a real estate agent in a small city in the rural area of São Paulo. Although he was illiterate, he was able to negotiate and deal with his clients, I believe, because of his hard work, good nature, and wisdom. If there was a discussion about religion with his family or friends, my grandpa would say, "There is no need to discuss, God is big and enough for everyone."

My grandfather's story of resilience, hard work, and achievement—including the fact that he came from a black family and married a white woman and had mixed descendants—is very common in Latin America. The region is vast, with abundant and fertile land. However, throughout the centuries it has been exploited and it has been a place of fights for natural resources, such as minerals, wood, water, and plantations. Only recently have Latin American people started to enjoy the richness of the land, overcome the historical inequalities, and improve life for everyone in the continent.

As a Brazilian and a Latin American, writing this book gave me an extraordinary opportunity to immerse myself in my origins and learn about the people in my country. I took on the writing as an opportunity to share our history, our view, and perspective with others. Latin America is a huge territory, around 21,000,000 km², (7,412,000 sq. mi), almost 3.7 percent of the earth's surface or 12.9 percent of its land surface area. As of 2013, its population was estimated at more than 618 million.[1] For several months, I was immersed in extensive research of historical articles, books, interviews, previous Methodist studies on the region, and papers, about our history, achievements, challenges, religion, and culture, which is reflected in these pages. But my main discovery was about the people. Writing this study helped me gain a new perspective about my people in Latin America. How strong, faithful, and resilient we are. Even though we have faced so many challenges for centuries, our people are proud of our land, economy, music, festivities, and our joy.

Latin America Facts and People

Latin America consists of South America, Central America, the Caribbean; it spans more than one continent. The term "Latin America" has been used since the nineteenth century to name the countries of the region that were primarily colonized by Spain and Portugal, but also by France, Great Britain, and the Netherlands. So, the name Latin America not only relates to a region, but also refers to a great number of countries whose primary languages—Portuguese and Spanish—share a common root. Geographically, South America, Central America, parts of the Caribbean islands, and part of North America form the region.

South America: Argentina, Bolivia, Brazil, Chile, Colombia, Ecuador, Guyana, Paraguay, Peru, Suriname, Uruguay, and Venezuela

Central America: Belize, Costa Rica, El Salvador, Guatemala, Honduras, Nicaragua, and Panama

North America: Mexico

Caribbean: Cuba, Dominican Republic, Haiti, Jamaica, and other small islands.

Latin America is bordered by the Atlantic Ocean on the east and by the Pacific Ocean on the west. It is a region known for its natural resources, such as the Amazon rainforest, where nearly half of all the earth's species exist. It is a place of extensive mountain ranges with mineral deposits in the Andean region, plenty of fertile agricultural areas, including the Pampas (plains) of Argentina and Uruguay, desolate spaces, such as the Atacama Desert in Chile, the beautiful shores of the Caribbean Sea, and of friendly and festive people.

This book is the result of considerable research and intends to present Latin America in a broad perspective with a historical and sociocultural overview of the continent. As the subject is so wide and complex, it is divided into five chapters.

Chapter 1 presents the historical process of colonization, and the life and culture of pre-Columbian civilizations, including the Aztecs, Mayans, Incas, and Tupi-Guarani. It also presents the diversity of its people formed by the encounter of two different worlds—the original inhabitants of the region and the European colonists, and the millions of enslaved people brought over from Africa (the region was the main destination for the African slave trade).

Chapter 2 presents the periods of independence during the eighteenth century, the immigration waves of the late nineteenth and early twentieth centuries, and the nations' efforts to develop their new political, economic, social, and cultural statuses.

Chapter 3 focuses on presenting the main challenges that Latin America is is currently facing by looking back to the historical foundations and the relationships with international political powers. It examines the initiatives that have been taking place to overcome those challenges.

Chapter 4 presents the importance of popular culture—Latin American music, dance, literature, and art, and the role women play in those fields—as well as in media and politics. Besides the hard time of resistance during the dictatorship period, the focus is on the recent shift towards democracy, and how women have been consistently part of the political scene.

Chapter 5 presents the role of the church in Latin America: how religion has been influenced by the people; how it has been sometimes connected to the powerful and political establishment; and how at times it has provided support and hope to the poor. This chapter also explores how Latin Americans have been affected and influenced by the different religions and beliefs of those who came to the land as immigrants, and finally a offers historical perspective of the Methodist Church in the region.

Above all, this book aims to present an overview of the richness of Latin America and its people for readers in the North American continent.

As a black Latin American woman from Brazil, I tried to present an insider's view, sharing our history, challenges, hopes, joys, and how, in spite of our historical difficulties, we still have faith in the future and are working to improve our region for all the people. I also tried to highlight many of the great women who gave their lives to build a better land for their children, through their work, art, and politics.

To reflect our Latin American spirit, I have included two personal profiles at the end of each chapter. These are interviews with men and women of different ages, most of them Brazilian, but also a Portuguese and a Peruvian immigrant. They have different professions, backgrounds, and experiences. The idea is to present what daily life in Brazil is like for a musician, a journalist, an indigenous healer, and an ecumenical activist who was imprisoned and tortured during the dictatorship period, as well as a Brazilian journalist of Japanese ancestry, and others. The intent of the profiles is to illustrate the range of similarities and differences of Latin Americans by focusing on the daily life experiences of these people.

In conclusion, I hope this book will encourage reflection, discussion, and a broader view of Latin American people and the land, our richness and challenges, our faith, achievements and difficulties, our endeavors and joy, and the beauty of our people.

I'll be very glad if this book could also stimulate curiosity and interest for the world at large to recognize that Latin America has its own unique context and history. The people who live here and those from other parts of the world are children of the same humanity and together, with faith, respect and solidarity, can build a better place for everybody.

So, you are my guest and you are invited to make a reading journey to Latin America.

Welcome!

Endnotes

1. "America – Latin America and Caribbean," *Population Reference Bureau*, 2014 Data Sheet, www.prb.org/DataFinder/Geography/Data.aspx?loc=313.

Soli Marita, a three-year-old Wichí indigenous girl, runs through the forest near her home in Lote 75, an indigenous neighborhood of Embarcación, Argentina.
(Paul Jeffrey)

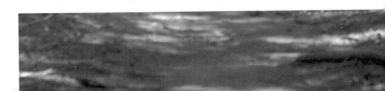

A young man in San Salvador stands in front of a streetside mural he helped to paint. It is part of a project sponsored by Quetzalcoatl, a Salvadoran nongovernmental organization. *(Paul Jeffrey)*

Chapter 1

Encounter of Two Civilizations

People in the New Continent

Before the colonization period, around 57 million people from many different ethnic groups inhabited Latin America. These groups had their own social and political organization, language, and religion. A great mixture of people with strong and long history lives in Latin America. They are very different from each other in appearance as well as in lifestyle, culture, beliefs, and way of thinking.

There are many discussions about the correct term for the original inhabitants of Latin America. It is said that when Christopher Columbus arrived in the Antilles, he called the inhabitants "Indians," because he thought that he had reached the Indian Ocean. Although Columbus' mistake was recognized, the term "indigenous" continues to be used to refer to all the original inhabitants of Latin America.

In North America, the original inhabitants came to be called Native American, with ample acceptance, but the peoples from other Latin America regions continued to be called indigenous. And also the term "indigenous" has predominated as a generic term to define many groups as tribes, first peoples/nations, aboriginals, or ethnic groups. At times, it also has been used for some occupational and geographical terms like hunter-gatherers, nomads, peasants, hill people, etc., and for all practical purposes can be used in the place of "indigenous peoples."

More recently, the United Nations proposed a more broad understanding about the term that should be used to denominate peoples with some characteristic as practicing unique traditions and who retain social, cultural, economic, and political aspects that are distinct from those of the dominant societies in which they live. These populations can be found spread across the world from the Arctic to the South Pacific, as descendants—according to a common definition—of those who inhabited a country or a geographical region at the time when people of different cultures or ethnic origins arrived. "Among the indigenous peoples are those of the Americas (for example, the Lakota in the USA, the Mayas in Guatemala or the Aymaras in Bolivia), the Inuit and Aleutians of the circumpolar region, the Saami of northern Europe, the Aborigines and Torres Strait Islanders of Australia and the Maori of New Zealand. These and most other indigenous peoples have retained distinct characteristics which are clearly different from those of other segments of the national populations."[1]

Historians have said that the people of the Americas probably began to arrive approximately 30,000 years ago when climatic changes permitted migration from Siberia across the Bering Strait. As Freddy Delgado and Felipe Gomez affirm:

> It took another 8,000 years for these small wandering human bands to reach the southern edge of the continent, Patagonia, and to spread throughout Central and South America. Those who adapted to the Amazon Basin continued in a hunter-gatherer mode, learning the skills needed to survive in a tropical rain forest.

Agriculture arose simultaneously in the Andean highlands and in Central Mexico some 5,000 years ago, first as a supplement to hunting and gathering, and later as a response to growing populations.

The teosinte, a high protein precursor of corn, was first cultivated in Mexico, while potato was an early ecologically-adapted crop in the colder Andes. The list of cultivated edible plants soon expanded to include manioc, maize, squash, peppers, pineapple, and other American originals, especially several varieties of beans.[2]

> *The indigenous groups in Latin America believe that when humans respect their natural environment and adapt themselves to it, nature will maintain its equilibrium and supply them with what they need. When humans take care and respect the different spiritual forces, as well as conduct properly the rituals and sacrifices, these forces will remain quiet and will offer them protection, support, and abundance.[3]*

With economic, social, and cultural mores based in local crops, restricted markets, and a religion that pledges a very respectful relation to nature, the arrival of the Europeans had a huge impact on the indigenous peoples. Although these communities are varied, with similar as well as differentiating characteristics, it is important to have an overview of Latin American history and populations before the colonization period. Considering the wide variety of civilizations, it is necessary to restrict our focus on only some of them. Four are presented here to gain a broad perspective of the rich history of American peoples during the pre-Columbian period.

The Aztecs

Some history scholars say that the Aztecs or *Mejicas,* as they named themselves, left North America around the twelfth century in search of fertile land, and after a long journey arrived at Anahuac Valley (today, the Valley of Mexico) and founded the city of Tenochtitlán, its capital. The Aztecs built a powerful and rich empire that extended from Central Mexico to Guatemala, El Salvador, and Honduras.

According to many scholars, it was common among pre-Columbian peoples to have a strong belief in female power. The Aztecs believed that women's involvement was essential in creating a well-balanced and ordered society. "Believing the balance between men and women was essential to a well-functioning society, pre-Columbian Aztec communities provided women with social, religious, and political power, making them significant and, in many cases, equal contributors to Aztec social world," notes scholar Rhianna C. Rogers.[4] Even for the purpose of inheritance, both men and women were entitled to own and inherit property as well as enjoy social status based on kinship and lineages.

In both rural and urban settings, women were expected to regulate activities within the private domain (e.g., getting married and raising children) as well as pay imperial tribute. More specifically, all women were required to pay tribute in the form of cloth and woven goods to the imperial Aztec state.

When the Spanish arrived in America, Tenochtitlán was a city of around 200,000 people, four times the size of London, the biggest city in Europe at that time. The Aztecs had a city with streets, temples, and a central market, along with aqueducts and a water distribution system. Despite its resistance, Tenochtitlán was conquered by the Spanish in 1521.

The Maya

Another important pre-Columbian civilization, the Maya lived on the Yucatán Peninsula, currently the area of Guatemala, Honduras, Belize, and South Mexico. The Mayans were great builders who constructed palaces and temples in pyramid form, many of which exist today. Among the crops they cultivated were beans, avocados, and corn.

Based on their study of the movement of celestial bodies, the Mayans developed a calendar that even today is considered extremely accurate, and could predict solar and lunar eclipses. Mayan astronomers observed and recorded the phases of Venus, which is believed to have influenced their decisions to go to war.

In Mayan society, women were considered equal to men and not subordinate to them. However, they had different duties and responsibilities than the men: taking care of household activities such as preparing food, bringing water, gathering firewood, processing dried corn into flour. Mayan women also participated in governmental and economic activities; some were known to have even ruled over kingdoms, such as Ix Wac Chaan Ahau who conquered several cities in the region of El Naranjo, Mexico.[5]

The Inca

The Inca people flourished in the area where Peru is today. They survived on agriculture and herding. The main cities of their empire were Cuzco and Machu Picchu. The Inca empire was vast, stretching from what today is the border of Colombia in the north to the northern areas of Chile and Argentina in the south. Machu Picchu, believed to have been built as a retreat for one of the Incan emperors around 1450 AD, is located in the mountains, at about 2,400 meters (8,000 ft.). Its construction still intrigues archeologists, given that the Incas did not use wheels or strong draft animals to haul the massive stones used in the structures up the steep terrain to the site.

The Incas developed agriculture and effective irrigation systems. In Inca society, women were mainly responsible for taking care of children, cooking, and all household activities.

The Incas are considered to have been polytheist, and thus worshipped many gods. In general, they related to celestial bodies—the earth, the moon, and the sun—and believed that they descended from the sun god and the moon. To ensure their wellbeing, it was incumbent on the Incas to please the gods through making sacrifices to them. They also venerated many features of natural and human made landscapes, including the buildings, shrines, and towers that they erected, some of which can still be found in the region of Peru.

The Tupi-Guarani

Another indigenous group in South America is known as the Tupi-Guarani, a term used for various Indigenous communities who inhabited the coastal region of Brazil. It is believed that the origin of these groups was the Amazon rainforest and by 500 BC, they began to spread throughout the continent. They had a similar language and similar way of living: in groups of 500 to 3,000 people in wood houses. The Tupi-Guarani had a system of distributed power and the main decisions were made after consultation with the elders of the group. Most of the Tupi-Guarani people were destroyed by the arrival of the Portuguese colonizers, mainly because they didn't show much resistance at first, and when they did they were beaten. They were considered very peaceful people.

Tupi-Guarani women cooked and took care of children, and also farmed and fished. The women were in charge of making fishing nets, baskets, and other handcrafts. It is important to note the role of Tupi-Guarani women during the Portuguese colonization in Brazil. The miscegenation (racial mixing) among Portuguese settlers and Tupi-Guarani women started when the Portuguese first arrived. As the Portuguese colonists rarely brought women from Europe, indigenous women were made a "breeding matrix of Brazilian people" as the Brazilian anthropologist Darcy Ribeiro calls it. He affirmed that the Tupi-Guarani had a tradition of incorporating strangers into their community by offering a tribal girl as wife; this was called "cunhadismo" (from the Portuguese word "cunhado," meaning brother-in-law). Once the Portuguese colonist agreed, he formed a bond of kinship with all the people of the tribe.[6]

Another common practice among the indigenous people was polygamy that was quickly adopted by the Portuguese settlers; a single European colonist could have many indigenous wives. By this practice, the colonist could have many relatives in an indigenous community, and then use this kinship to recruit natives to work.

Arrival of Columbus to the New Land

The colonization of America started in 1492 during a period of great discoveries in Europe. With the support of the king and queen of Spain, Fernando de Aragón and Isabel of Castilla, Christopher Columbus set sail from the port of Palos de la Frontera in Spain with three vessels (Santa Maria, Pinta, and Niña). After sailing for two months, he found the "new" continent: America. It was October 12, 1492, and Columbus arrived in the region today called the Bahamas in the Caribbean. As he thought he had arrived in India, he named the different people who had inhabited the land for thousands of years, "Indians." There is controversy about Columbus' arrival. Was his landing a discovery, an encounter, or an invasion? Some academics disagree about the hypothesis of discovery because when Columbus arrived, there were millions of indigenous peoples already on the American continent. Others, including Miguel Leon de Portilla, suggest that it was a two-world encounter, one that was between the European and the American worlds. And then there are scholars who affirm that due to the number of indigenous deaths, October 12, 1492, should be considered a day of invasion.

After Columbus arrived, many other Europeans followed him, including Portuguese Pedro Álvares Cabral, who commanded a squad of vessels in 1500 to the land known today as Brazil. After Cabral, English, French, and Dutch navigators followed.

The Colonization in America

When the Spanish officer Hernán Cortés arrived at what is today called Mexico, he had 508 soldiers, as well as horses and cannons. The news about the arrival of these white men with iron clothes and mounted on strange animals (the Aztecs didn't know horses) and bearing firearms frightened the natives. Even Montezuma, the Aztec emperor, thought Cortés was an Aztec god because they had a myth about the god that would come from the sea. He offered many gifts but Cortés and his soldiers didn't want friendship. They took Montezuma prisoner and began their path

of conquest by taking the gold from the Aztecs. After many battles and alliances with the Aztecs' enemies, Cortés invaded Tenochititlan and ended the Aztec empire in 1521.

Another Spanish adventurer, Francisco Pizarro, was also eager to find gold in America and turned his attention to the Inca Empire. He also made alliances with the Inca's enemies and invaded the main city, Cuzco, and arrested the Inca king Atahualpa in 1532. The Incas fought back and their wars lasted until 1572, when Túpac Amaru, the last Inca, was arrested and decapitated.

There are historical accounts of indigenous resistance to colonization, in places such as the Yucatán Peninsula, the Peruvian Amazon region, and the Andean highlands, which had suffered a severe depopulation. Studies have also documented revolts in other places, such as Vilcabamba in Peru, where the rebels were able to establish a "liberated zone."[7] Other major insurgencies also broke out in Ecuador in 1578, 1599, and 1615.

But the indigenous people's fight for their lands was a very unequal one. They had to defend themselves without adequate firepower and lacked preparation to defeat such strong invaders. We need to consider that the firearms used by the European conquerors caused many deaths but the diseases brought by the Europeans killed just as many, perhaps more. Diseases, including tuberculosis and smallpox, killed thousands of indigenous people very quickly; first, because they had no natural immunity to these diseases and, second, because these diseases manifested in epidemics, affecting people from the same group, so they had no access to proper treatment.

Spanish America: Source of Richness

The discovery of the new continent was a source of dispute for European countries. Scholars have divided the colonization in America into two parts depending upon the aim of the colonists. The colonization by settlers in North America was characterized mostly by family-based settlements, with people wanting to create a new life in a new land. On the other hand, the main objective of the European colonists in Latin America was to exploit the new land—including extracting gold and minerals—and returning to their home country with the spoils.

At the beginning of the seventeenth century, the Spanish were spreading through the islands of the Caribbean, in Florida in North America, and throughout the southern Western Hemisphere, establishing numerous settlements, which included mines, ranches, and plantations. Portugal concentrated its colonization endeavors in Brazil. Other European countries attempted to establish colonies. In 1604, the French occupied the island of Guadeloupe. Occupation of Martinique, Haiti and various smaller Caribbean islands, and what is today called French Guiana, soon followed. Meanwhile, England colonized Honduras and Jamaica. The Dutch were present in the Caribbean (Aruba, Curaçao, and Bonaire) in what today is referred to the Netherland Antilles. Guyana, on the northeastern coast of South America, was originally colonized by the Dutch. Later, it became a British colony (British Guiana) and remained so for over 200 years until it achieved independence from the United Kingdom on May 26, 1966. Bordering Guyana to the east, Suriname was colonized by the Dutch and English in the seventeenth century and then captured by the Dutch in 1667 (Dutch Guiana). It eventually became independent in 1975 as Suriname.

Life in the Spanish American Colonies

The discovery of rich silver mines in Potosí (Bolivia today), and in Zacatecas (Mexico today), among other sources of gold indicate that during the first 250 years of Spanish presence in America, the main activity was mining. Indigenous people were forced to work in the mines according to the system of *mit'a* and *encomienda*. *Mit'a* was an ancient Inca practice of mandatory public service for the sake of the Incan Empire. The Spanish crown adapted this (*mit'a*), allowing colonists to recruit indigenous people for forced labor. *Encomienda* granted the Spanish colonist the right to exact tribute of either gold or labor (mostly mining) from the indigenous people of the area. In exchange, the colonist was required to protect the indigenous people from warring tribes and to instruct them in the Spanish language and Christian religion. In practice, the difference between *encomienda* and slavery was minimal, many indigenous people were forced to do hard labor and faced extreme punishment and even death if they resisted. Consequently, thousands of indigenous people died under this system.

For the most part, the Hispanic-American society consisted of a minority of criollos—white people of European descent born in the new lands, with riches and power—and a majority of indigenous people, mestizos, and African slaves who provided unpaid or underpaid labor. The indigenous people, Africans, and mestizos also suffered strong racial discrimination.

Mining in Bolivia

One example of the exploitation of natural resources of Latin America in the 1700s was the mining in Potosí, Bolivia, located at 4000m (13,000 ft.) above sea level. During its golden years, Potosí became one of the richest and largest cities in the world with a population exceeding 200,000 during the sixteenth and the eighteenth centuries. Initially, indigenous people were forced to labor in the mines but exposure to European diseases, the use of mercury (metal used to separate the gold), and their brutal mistreatment decimated the population. Consequently, and due to the economic benefits gained from slave trade, African slaves were brought to Potosí. As the living and work conditions were the worst possible, a slave's life span could be as short as two months, and so slaves were deemed cost effective.

The African slaves made an important connection with the indigenous people who shared their knowledge and expertise of the countryside. At times, some were even able to escape from the deplorable living conditions of enslavement and forced labor.

Portuguese Colonization

The first Portuguese colonists didn't find any gold or silver in Brazil, but they found the Brazilwood tree (*Caesalpina echinata*), an important source of red dye. Soon, the French started to come to Brazil to exploit the Brazilwood tree. The Portuguese, realizing the difficulty of defending such an extended coast, decided to occupy the land.

During the sixteenth century, Brazilian sugarcane became the leading crop. Since there were few Portuguese colonists—they considered themselves gentlemen unsuited for the hard labor of work in the cane fields—they tried to use indigenous people as their main workforce. But the indigenous people resisted their land's occupation and the attempts of forced labor. Many killed the Portuguese or escaped into the forest or interior. As a result, the Portuguese deemed the indigenous people unsuited for plantation work. On the other hand, the Portuguese African slaves provided a great economic solution because the slave trade was very profitable. Some African people knew iron metallurgy and had experience in sugarcane plantations; the Portuguese were already using African slaves in Portugal, so they started to import them to Brazil in the sixteenth century.

The Role of the Roman Catholic Church During the Colonial Period

During the colonization, the influence of Catholic Church was immense. By the right of patronage (*patronato),* which was a series of treaties and arrangements between the Pope and the kings of Spain and Portugal, those who discovered the lands became legitimate owners. In exchange, the kings facilitated the exportation of the Catholic faith to the new lands. In fact, this system effectively allowed Portugal and Spain to colonize Latin America, exploit its richness, and in many ways justified their conquest as the church endeavored to convert indigenous people and Africans.

Historians say that the church held the role of maintaining social order in a new society of so many different kinds of people, Europeans, indigenous, Africans, and mestizos. The historian Charles Boxer noted that missionaries were sent with the primary responsibility to pacify the frontiers; they were escorted by soldiers, if needed. Once an area was suitably resettled in villages and laity appointed, the missionaries would move to a new area.[8]

The church's influence included its support and justification of the forced conversion of indigenous and African peoples to Catholicism and slavery, promoting that should obey their owners because by so doing they would be rewarded in heaven. But it was not a unanimous position. One of these voices was Fray Bartolomé de Las Casas (1474–1566), who is considered a defender of all indigenous peoples, as he called himself; he dedicated his life to denounce the abuses of Spanish colonization.

Some of these church voices were ambiguous. For example, Father Antonio Vieira, who spoke in his sermons against slavery and indigenous forced labor, said that he didn't approve that slaves should be treated with cruelty and criticized slave owners who behaved in such a way, but he did not speak out against the institution of slavery itself.[9] In fact, in his sermons he said that the slaves should obey their masters in all respects regardless of the way they are treated, and that what happens on earth was not important but the slaves should think about the rewards they would gain in heaven.[10]

To a great extent, through the influence of the Catholic Church, family bonds among slaves were fostered and encouraged. Up to two-thirds of all adult slaves in Colombia lived in family units, and parents had rights over the fate of their children—when sale occurred, it was more often than not the sale of families. Almost the same thing happened in other countries in Latin America, including Brazil and Bolivia.

Slavery in Latin America

It is estimated that 12 million Africans were shipped as slaves to North America, the Caribbean, and South America, during the sixteenth, seventeenth, eighteenth, and nineteenth centuries. History of slavery in Latin

America involved a complex connection of interests, including political and economic, and the vast exploitation of land over several centuries.

The slaves represented a variety of different cultures and societies; they were followers of traditional African religions, but some were Muslim. Slaves were shipped across the Atlantic under very harsh conditions. They were held in crowded ships and treated brutally. It is estimated that over the years a total of 2.5 million died during the journey.

In Colombia the major destination for slave ships was the town of Cartagena at the port of Nueva Granada. The African slaves started to arrive by the 1520s to replace the declining indigenous population. Cartagena also served as a hub for the Latin American slave trade, where slaves were sold to go on to various destinations in the Andes and beyond. Within Colombia, slaves carried out a wide range of tasks: They were muleteers (*tropeiros*), cowboys, blacksmiths, domestic servants, gold miners, pearl divers; they worked on sugarcane, tobacco, and cotton cultivation in the haciendas (the Spanish word for plantation or farms).

Many slaves in Latin America fought for their freedoms, and they happened to build strong free black African towns called *palenques*, where Africans could live as free men and women. African people played key roles in the independence struggle against Spain. Historians note that three of every five soldiers in Simon Bolívar's army were African. Not only that, Afro-Colombians also participated at all levels of military and political life.

Brazil was the last country to end the slavery that lasted until 1888. It has been estimated that from the sixteenth to the nineteenth centuries, a total of 3.6 million African slaves were brought to Brazil compared to 500,000 who were sent to the United States. By the middle of the seventeenth century, it was said that the slave population in Brazil was more numerous than the free population. At that time, life expectancy was much lower for everyone than today, but it calls to our attention that a Brazilian slave had a life expectancy of nineteen years, in contrast to the thirty-five years for a slave in the United States.[11]

The main crop in Brazil was the sugarcane produced by the *engenhos* (sugar cane mill), which encompassed the sugarcane crop cultivation and production, and included the hacienda and the *senzala* (the slaves' homes). Most white children were raised by black nannies, and the price of a slave was low, so even a poor Brazilian had at least one slave.

In Latin America in general, but in Brazil in particular, there was a great deal of racial mixing; first, because white women were rare in the colony, and because Portuguese culture was less rigid about it; and for the most part, the Spanish and Portuguese didn't acknowledge their mulatto offspring, what the mixed descendants were called.

There were many forms of slave resistance; one was called Capoeira, a combination of dancing and fight, which was used as an entertainment and defense. Capoeira is still an important Afro-Brazilian cultural expression. The slaves also disobeyed their masters by not working hard, breaking their tools, burning their crops, being aggressive, escaping, and even committing suicide.

In Brazil, the resistance groups created settlements called quilombos *that existed all over the country. The largest that lasted the longest was the Quilombo dos Palmares from 1597 to 1695. During the seventeenth century it had 15,000 people, who were well-organized, and had their own crops and production. Besides former African slaves, in Palmares there also lived poor white men and indigenous people who had been expelled from their land. Their main leader was Zumbi, who led them to rise against many plantation owners and the Portuguese and Brazilian authorities. After almost after a century, the local authorities, with superior weaponry, managed to defeat them and Zumbi was killed on November 20, 1695. This date became the resistance symbol, and now it's called the National Day of Black Consciousness.*

by diseases brought by the Europeans and their harsh mistreatment. During the seventeenth century, the French occupied the entire island and called it Saint-Domingue. By this time, a massive influx of African slaves had come to the island and Saint-Domingue becoming one of the richest French colonies in the world.

There was a huge social and economic gap between the white elite and the slave workers. Reacting to their oppression by the colonists, in 1791 the black slaves led by Toussaint L'Ouverture started one of the biggest rebellions in Latin America. They conquered the eastern side of the island with a small army of rebels, and abolished slavery. Soon after, L'Overture was captured and sent to France where he died in prison. But, the fight for freedom continued and a new leader arose. Jean Jacques Dessalines defeated the French and declared the independence of Haïti, which in 1804 was the second country in America to become independent after the United States.

Independence Processes in Latin America

The processes by which Latin American countries gained their independence took place over many years. All had been subjected to crises resulting from failure of colonialism. During the eighteenth century, the colonies were exhausted by high taxes, restrictions on the production of their own products, enormous social and economic inequities, discrimination, and the inequitable distribution of privileges to the governors to the detriment of the colonists. In the meantime, there was great turmoil in Europe. The French Revolution and the ideas of equality, freedom, and fraternity were spreading. In North America, the thirteen British colonies had won a war of independence from Great Britain.

The Independence of Haiti

The land where Haiti is today was a part of the island of Hispaniola, where Columbus landed in 1492. Within decades the native population was nearly decimated

The independence struggle in northern South America began in 1806, when Venezuelan Francisco de Miranda first attempted to liberate his homeland with British help. This attempt failed, but Miranda returned in 1810 to head up the first Venezuelan Republic with Simon Bolívar and others. Bolívar fought the Spanish in Venezuela, Ecuador, and Colombia for many years, decisively beating them several times. By 1822, those countries were free, and Bolívar set his sights on Peru, the last and mightiest Spanish holdout on the continent.[12]

The fights were intense and had spread all over the continent. Liberty armies lead by José de San Martín started by freeing Argentina (1816) and Chile (1818), and then continued to march into Peru.

The Independence of Peru

By the end of the eighteenth century, indigenous and mestizo rebellions sprouted in Peru including the rebellion led by José Gabriel Condorcanqui, who changed his name to Túpac Amaru II, the same name as the last Inca king. The Spanish later defeated him. He and his spouse, who had fought by his side, were executed.

Although Túpac Amaru II's rebellion was not a success, it marked the first large-scale rebellion in the Spanish colonies and inspired the revolt of many natives and mestizos in the surrounding area. The rebellion took on important manifestations in the highlands of "Upper Peru," or what today is modern Bolivia, including the Southeast region of Lake Titicaca.

In the meantime, another great criollo leader, Simón Bolívar, led a rebel army liberating and gaining independence for the region called the Gran Colombia (Colombia, Venezuela, Panama, and Ecuador) becoming its president.

Simón Bolívar (1783–1830) was the greatest leader of Latin America's independence movement from Spain. Bolívar, a superb general and a charismatic politician, not only drove the Spanish from northern South America but also was instrumental in the early formative years of the republics that sprang up once the Spanish had gone. His later years are marked by the collapse of his grand dream of a united South America. He is remembered as "The Liberator," the man who liberated his home from Spanish rule.

Bolívar entered world history as one of the first modern leaders of a national liberation movement. His ambition was to unite rather than divide the Spanish American peoples. He created the great state of Colombia (Gran Colombia), comprised of Colombia, Venezuela, Panama, and Ecuador. He then sought to unite this with Peru and Bolivia in a Federation of the Andes. And he dreamed of the "great day of America" when its peoples would come together in a league of nations.

The Independence of Mexico

In Mexico, two priests, Miguel Hidalgo and José Maria Morelos, were among the leaders of the movement to win independence from Spain. Their first attempts were defeated by the Spanish troops and Hidalgo was captured and executed in 1811. Colonel Agustín Iturbide, a royalist supporting the independence movement, assumed leadership and declared Mexico's independence in 1821.

Independence in Mexico was sparked by Father Miguel Hidalgo, a priest living and working in the small town of Dolores in the state of Guanajuato. He and a small group of conspirators started the rebellion by ringing the church bells on the morning of September 16. This act became known as the "Cry of Dolores." His ragtag army made it partway to Mexico City before being driven back, and Hidalgo himself was captured and executed in July of 1811.

With Hidalgo gone, the Mexican independence movement almost failed, but another priest who was also a talented field marshal—José María Morelos—assumed command. Morelos won a series of impressive victories against Spanish forces before being captured and executed in December 1815.

The Independence of Brazil

Brazil was also part of the rebellions of the seventeenth, eighteenth, and nineteenth centuries. In 1808, Portugal's King John VI, the royal family, and his court arrived in Brazil escaping from Napoleon's troops. This opened up the possibility for an independent country. The king's arrival encouraged free trade and stimulated subsequent prosperity. When the king returned to Europe, his son, Dom Pedro, was left to become the ruler prince. Napoleon had been defeated; it was the right

A Mam-speaking Maya woman weaves using a traditional backstrap loom in the village of San Martín Chile Verde in Guatemala. *(Paul Jeffrey)*

time to gain the allegiance of local elite groups to begin the process of independence. Dom Pedro was appointed leader, becoming Pedro I, and proclaimed Brazil's independence in 1822.

Dominant groups, including landowners and successful traders, led the Brazilian independence process. Although the poor people and slaves had started rebellions and resistance movements, they did not participate in the final process of independence.

The Role of Women During Independence

During the colonial period, only men were seen in the army. It is easy to forget that women also participated in many ways in the independence wars. It is important to highlight how women also participated in the fighting for independence. Most of them followed their husbands or sons who were soldiers; they worked beside them with the food supplies, cooking, washing, and sewing. Some of them were spies or participated in supporting activities, including printing and distribution of independent pamphlets.

Maria Ligia Prado, from the University of São Paulo in Brazil, is a scholar specializing in Latin America and tells about many women who were part of the Independence Movements. One of these women was from Argentina, Deolinda Correa, who is known by her nickname "Difunta Correa" (Deceased Correa). The legend is that she was a young woman with a baby who accompanied her husband as a soldier during the fights against federalists. Due to the struggles in the campaign and the lack of supplies, she died. It is said that when her body was found, the baby was still alive. It had been feeding from the deceased woman's breast. By this legend, Difunta Correa became a popular saint in the region.

Prado also talks about Maria Quitéria de Jesus, a Brazilian woman who came from a humble family in Bahia. In order to be a part of the Brazilian War of Independence, she cut her hair and dressed as a man for the first time. After a while she was discovered, but when she gained recognition, because of her courage she was promoted to cadet, then lieutenant, and even decorated with the Imperial Order.

It's important to mention Policarpa Salavarrieta, also known as "La Pola," who is considered a heroine in Colombia. She worked as a dressmaker at the houses of the royalist elitist Spanish community. She was able to gather valuable information about the war that she passed to her fiancé, who was part of the revolutionary forces during the Spanish reconquest of the Viceroyalty of Nueva Granada, which is currently Colombia. She was captured by the Spanish and executed for high treason.

Another woman mentioned by Prado is Javiera Carrera, who is called "Mother of Chile," and belonged to an established traditional family. She, along with her brothers José Miguel, Juan José, and Luis, actively participated in the Chilean War of Independence. They were some of most important leaders of the early Chilean struggle for independence during the period known as the Patria Vieja ("Old Republic"). She is credited with having sewn the first national flag of Chile and she is considered to be the "Mother of Chile."[13]

Wichí indigenous children study in a school in El Algarrobal, a small town in the Chaco region of northern Argentina. *(Paul Jeffrey)*

Profiles

Carlos Seabra

Carlos Seabra, a Portuguese born in Lisbon, migrated to Brazil as a teenager in the 1960s. His parents chose to live in Brazil because of their love of Brazilian music. "My parents met at the College of Fine Arts, and their friends were writers, musicians, people who opposed the dictatorial regime in Portugal at the time. We used to listen to lots of Brazilian music at home. There was a Finnish woman who would come with her guitar and play bossa nova tunes and songs like 'O Barquinho' (Little Boat)[...all] are part of my childhood."

When he was 14, Seabra came to Brazil to live and work with his father, who had an advertising agency. He got a job as a designer and enjoyed the editorial field; he worked as an art and iconographic research assistant in a small publishing company.

Seabra's wife was also born in Portugal. "In 1974, in Portugal, we started talking about the April 25 Revolution and while chatting, we started dating. After 40 years, now we have three children and three grandchildren. The eldest grandchild is 15 years old, the second is 12, and the little one is three years old."

Nowadays, Seabra works at Editora FTD, a traditional book publisher in Brazil, which is linked to the Catholic Church's Marianist group. There, he coordinates the production of digital material, games, audiovisuals, simulators, and online educational systems, for schoolbooks and literature books, among other products.

Seabra talks about a difficult moment he had in a previous job when he had to let go of some of his employees. He questions: "What criteria would you choose to fire people? Would you think of each particular situation? Or of those who earn the highest wages? Or the younger ones?" What had helped him decide? He says, "Being peaceful with yourself and be set in the ideas in which you believe. Not violating your principles, or your values. Even if you do things that go against what you would like to do."

Carlos is not religious; he claims to be atheist. But he lives well with all of the religions and redeems the sense of the word *religare*. "That's what I like. The human being is what matters to me in religion. It's a kind of politics." He is interested in the political issue of religion, its civilizing side and how people get organized. "I just don't believe in God."

"Dona" Francisca

"Dona" Francisca, this 59-year-old woman of indigenous origins, starts her day: greeting birds. "Good morning, my pretty birds. Good morning, Sun," she says. She lives in an indigenous community next to the city of Cruzeiro do Sul in the Amazon, in the North of Brazil bordering Peru. There, everyone in the family lives next to one another, her eleven children, fourteen grandchildren, and some of her ten siblings.

"Dona" Francisca is a professional midwife. She worked alongside her mother and delivered her first baby when she was 15 years old. "My sister and my sister-in-law were in labor at the same time. My mother went to assist one of them, and my brother called me: 'Francisquinha, come and deliver the other baby.' It was the first time that I carried a baby in my arms." From that day on, she started to join her mother and see the deliveries, until she could continue by herself. "Seeing babies being born is so beautiful. Two lives we are bringing to the world: the baby and the mother. For me, it's a loving, affectionate thing. It brings me health, peace, love, life." She has delivered more than 1,000 babies.

She travels from time-time, going to São Paulo for deliveries and to learn about healing rituals. She has also

Joseno Neaud, a member of Nouvel Etwal (Haitian Creole for "New Stars") dances on the beach in Jacmel, Haiti. Nouvel Etwal, based in the southern village of Mizak, is a dance and creative movement group comprised of 16 girls from ages 8 to 13. According to Valerie Mossman-Celestin, an organizer of the group, "Nouvel Etwal seeks to empowers girls to be self-confident and creative. The girls learn flexibility, discipline, and teamwork, lessons they also need for life. Nouvel Etwal promotes health, well-being, and enhanced self-worth. The girls are encouraged to live into a brighter future where girls and women are valued, educated, and have equal opportunity to achieve their potential." *(Paul Jeffrey)*

of the Thirteen Grandmothers" in South Dakota that occurred in 2007. It is a time when indigenous grandmothers from different countries in the world gather and share their knowledge and practices. She has already gone to visit them in Spain and Norway, and maybe she will go to Peru or Guatemala soon. Before that, her longest trip had been to Rio Branco, the capital city in the state of Acre, which is three-and-a-half hours from Cruzeiro do Sul by plane.*

She learned the healing rituals, all using plants and herbs, from her father, who was a shaman. For the snuff—a powdery substance made of herbs that is drawn up into the nostrils—she plants, picks, and dries herbs and tobacco. She also works with Kambô (a vaccine that uses a secretion extracted from a frog) and ayahuasca (a brew produced from plants). According to her, those treatments are used "to seek the health spirit of health in the sick person."

And when she has to face a difficult situation, what gives her strength? "It is nature. It's the ayahuasca, the Kambô, the herbs, but especially, the forest. In the forest, I feel peace and joy, and when we go into the forest and walk, we let out bad things we have within us, amuse ourselves, and cheer up. When I'm sick in spirit, I go there to pick plants and talk to them. Do you know the samaúma? It is a very tall, a very big tree in the forest. I talk to her and ask for strength."

*The Council of Thirteen Grandmothers is an international group of senior Native American indigenous women (grandmothers) with the objective of working with issues such as environment and human rights. To learn more, visit www.grandmotherscouncil.org and en.avozdasavos.org.

Endnotes

1. "Who are indigenous peoples?" United Nations Permanent Forum on Indigenous Issues, accessed May 23, 2013, www.un.org/esa/socdev/unpfii/documents/5session_factsheet1.pdf.

2. Ibid.

3. Freddy Delgado and Felipe Gomez, "Knowledge and Belief Systems in Latin America," accessed May 23, 2013, www.compasnet.org/blog/wp-content/uploads/2011/03/ARNS/arns_17.pdf.

4. Rhianna C. Rogers, "The Resilience of Aztec Women: A Case Study of Modern Aztec Myths," *Scientific Journals International: Journal of Humanities and Social Sciences*, vol. 1, issue 2 (June 2007), www.scientificjournals.org/journals2007/articles/1160.pdf.

5. Claudio Obregón Clarin, "Las Reinas y Reyes Mayas," *Literatura y Mundo Maya*, last modified May 13, 2010, literaturaymundomaya.blogspot.com.br/2010/05/las-reinas-y-reyes-mayas.html.

6. Darcy Ribeiro, *O Povo Brasileiro, A formacao e o sentido do Brasil*, 2ºd. ed. (São Paulo: Companhia das Letras, 1997), 81.

7. Silvia Rivera Cusicanqui, "Aymara Past, Aymara Future," *NACLA Report on the Americas*, vol. XXV, n. 3 (Dec. 1991): 20.

8. Charles R. Boxer, *A Igreja Militante e a Expansão Ibérica 1440-1770*, trad. Vera Maria Pereira (São Paulo: Companhia das Letras, 2007), 72.

9. Antonio Vieira, "Sermon on the First Sunday of Lent," *Colonial Latin America: A Documentary History,* edited by Kenneth Mills, William B. Taylor, and Sandra Lauderdale Graham (Lantham: SR Books, 2004), 230.

10. Ibid., 221.

11. "Slavery in Brazil," the Library of Congress, accessed July 6, 2013, international.loc.gov/intldl/brhtml/br-1/br-1-3-1.html#track1.

12. Christopher Minster, "Francisco de Miranda, Precursor of Latin American Independence," *About.com*, accessed October 20, 2014, latinamericanhistory.about.com/od/latinamericaindependence/a/09fmiranda.htm.

13. Maria Ligia Coelho Prado, "Em busca da participação das mulheres nas lutas pela independência política da América Latina," *Revista Brasileira de História*, v. 23/24, n. 23/24 (1992): 77–90.

Johnny Antesano, a four-year-old Guarani indigenous boy from Choroquepiao, a small village in Bolivia's Chaco region, looks at his mother, Yela Vilera. *(Paul Jeffrey)*

Tomas Rivero, a leader of the Union of Pilcomayo River Fishers, casts a net as he fishes on the Pilcomayo River outside of Villamontes, Bolivia. He is also an advocate for cleaning up the river which has been plagued by contamination from upstream mining and road construction. *(Paul Jeffrey)*

Chapter 2

A Long Way to Stability and Democracy

The twentieth century began in Latin America as a time to seek economic development, political independence, and stabilization. All countries in the continent struggled to build political autonomy and to overcome centuries of land exploitation and economic dependence. The dependence upon the colonist countries, especially Spain and Portugal, by different economic interests was, due to changes in the global economic environment, transferred to England and later to the United States and other developed European countries, making the Northern Hemisphere a dominant economic pole.

Such economic dependency had direct impact on the political life of the countries of Latin America. To ensure their interests, both England and the United States established alliances with the great landowners and the traditional oligarchies, which were opposed to the industrialization and modernization of the economy and society initiatives to overcome foreign domination.

The domain of the traditional oligarchies' populism was based on exporting their agricultural commodities, possession of extensive rural property, and a working system based on dependency between the landowners and the workers.

Arrival of European Immigrants

However, at the end of the nineteenth century, the population of some Latin American countries began to diversify. Countries such as Brazil, Argentina, Uruguay, and Chile began to receive increasing numbers of European immigrants. These immigrants were runaways from the conflicts preceding World War I,

World War II, and the socio-economic instabilities in Europe prior to those wars. At the same time, it was the beginning of the period of industrialization, accompanied by the increasing expansion of cities in Latin America.

Between the years 1890 and 1930, it is estimated that around 3.2 million immigrants arrived in Brazil, about one million each from Italy and Portugal, and the remaining from Spain, Germany, Russia, Japan, Austria, Syria, and Lebanon.[1] White, Catholic, Italian, Portuguese, and Spanish immigrants were preferred by the authorities and farmland owners.

Most of the new arrivals started small businesses such as shoemaking, tailoring, shop keeping, and grocery selling. Those who went to rural areas usually worked on farms cultivating coffee, or on small properties. Asian immigrants, mainly Japanese, went to rural areas to work in agriculture. The Japanese government paid the fare of those who migrated to Brazil. The immigrants from Syria, Lebanon, and Jews from different European countries arrived with small business experience and eventually opened shops and factories.

During the early twentieth century, the theories of pure race were dominant and there was a belief among the Brazilian elite that European people were superior to people of color. As a result of this belief, the idea of "whitening" (*embranquecimento*) developed—that through the miscegenation (mixing of races) of European immigrants with Brazilians of indigenous, African, and Afro-Indigenous ancestors the Brazilian population would eventually whiten and dark-skinned races be eradicated. One result of this idea was that Brazil encouraged the immigration of Europeans.

Argentina, Uruguay, and Chile also were destinations for many European people in the late nineteenth and early twentieth centuries. Argentina was a preferred destination for the Jews escaping persecution, making it the country with the largest Jewish population in Latin America. Argentina also received around 1.5 million Spanish and 1.4 million Italians, and other Europeans including Polish, Russian, French, German, Austrian, Portuguese, Greek, Ukrainian, Croatian, Czech, British, Dutch, Scandinavian, and immigrants from Middle Eastern countries, mainly Syria and Lebanon. As a result of the migratory influx, Argentina has the second-largest immigrant population in the world, 6.6 million. The country with the largest immigrant population is the United States, with 27 million.[2]

The Church in Latin America during the Colonial Period

The role of the church in Latin America will receive more attention in Chapter 5, and the historical presence and political influences of religion in the region will be explored. Here it is important to point out the presence of different Christians in the region and how it relates to immigration, mainly in terms of the growth of the Protestant Church in Latin America.

Although Catholicism was dominant in the continent, other Christian denominations started to develop mainly during the nineteenth century. However, the roots of Protestantism can be found with the arrival of a group of German missionaries, some of them Lutherans, to Venezuela and Brazil beginning around 1530 and 1550.[3]

There is also information about the Scottish Protestant presence in Panama that came with the expedition of William Paterson during the seventeenth century. Another factor that contributed to the spread of Protestantism was the arrival of adventurers who came to Latin America to work, and somehow managed to escape from the control of the Catholic Church.

Still, during the colonial period many European immigrants after their arrival in the new lands continued to profess their religion, like the Germans, the English Anglicans, and most recently in the nineteenth century, the American Confederates who had settled in Brazil.

There are reports and many stories about the initiatives by farmers and English Protestant landlords in the Caribbean in Antigua, Jamaica, Barbados, and St. Barts. In the southern part of South America called "Southern Cone," the arrival of missionaries to Rio de la Plata in Argentina was started in 1835 with the Methodist missionary Justin Spaulding. In Brazil, the start was 1867 with US missionaries arriving in Brazil around 1867 to the Rio de Janeiro region.[4]

The presence of the Protestant missionaries increased after the independence process of the Latin American countries. Meanwhile, religious freedom and tolerance increased. Other political and social problems also fostered the entering of new religious parallels during the weakening of the Catholic Church, which had been involved with the colonial and post-colonial political powers.

In Mexico, for example, groups of North American missionary societies began to work in Mexico during the latter part of nineteenth century, including the Northern Presbyterian Missionary Society (1872), the Methodist Episcopal Missionary Society (1873), and the Southern Methodist Episcopal Missionary Society (1873). Methodism arrived in Brazil as a strong missionary force. It is considered to have started in 1867 by J. E. Newman, under the recommendation of the Board of Missions. According to The Reverend Duncan Alexander Reily, the "first Hall of worship was a small thatch-covered house, of clod soil, where before there was a store." Newman raised his own funds, of course, working in agriculture with other American settlers, so as not to be dependent on the mission. Newman remained in Brazil for 24 years.[5]

Another factor that helped to spread Protestantism in Latin America was the work of the American and the British Bible Societies. Many of the evangelists traveled around the continent distributing Bibles among the people. Between 1804 and 1807, the British Bible Society published approximately 20,000 New Testaments in Portuguese that were distributed around the Brazilian coast. The American Bible Society had distributed around two million Bibles and New Testaments, which were well-received.[6]

An important historical moment for Protestantism in Latin America was the Congress of Panama that was held in February 1916. Historians regard this congress a reaction to the 1910 World Missionary Conference in Edinburgh, Scotland. The Panama Congress included the participation of 235 delegates from 44 North American missionary societies, one from Canada, five from Great Britain, and 27 from Latin America. The Panama Congress ended with the creation of seven committees spread throughout Latin America—Argentina, Brazil, Chile, Cuba, Puerto Rico, Mexico and Peru—which were responsible at the national level for literature production, education, and training of new priests. For Fabio Josgrilberg, a theologian and professor from Methodist University in São Paulo, the results of these conferences, as well as the survey of the situation in each country and the cooperation projects, reveal the political background and the emerging nationalist concerns in mission countries. They had served to strengthen the bonds of Latin American Protestantism and started political policy dialogue among missionaries in the north in relation to the south.[7]

Some theologians, such as Mendonça, state that one of the goals of the Panama Congress was to firm up the principle that mission should only include the non-Christian world in its goals. However, at the conclusion of the Congress, a recommendation was made that the missionaries should look for areas not served by the Catholic Church, especially among the indigenous peoples. After the Congress, the Brazilian Presbyterian priest, Erasmo Braga, one of the early ecumenical activists in the region, was charged to write an emblematic publication about the event. *Pan-Americanism: The Religious Aspect* was published in New York (1916) in Portuguese and Spanish.[8]

Early Twentieth Century: Political Phases in Latin America

Because of the historical legacy of colonialism, politics in Latin America has some particularities. One of those is the domination and prevalence of small groups of wealthy and social elites in leadership positions that were generally well-established and in well-paid positions. Thus, power was concentrated in the hands of a few, defined as an oligarchy (government or control by a small group of people). In most Latin American countries, politics was dominated by an oligarchy based on exporting agricultural crops. As owners of extensive rural properties, the farmland owners and rich businessmen were the ones who became mayors and senators, and served in other places of power.

This kind of political system became more oppressive because it was associated with the continuation of slavery, reducing the possibilities of mobility and improvement among the poor. The system created a vicious cycle in that a worker's job was dependent on the relationship between the worker and landlord. In Brazil, for example, some of the manifestations of these relationships were called "clientelism." A system of favor exchange in which powerful people called "colonels" selected people who were called "clients" to whom they bestowed favors (often job opportunities), and in turn the clients became liable to the colonel and had to comply with his demands, which were often exploitive.

In the late nineteenth century, there were some who started to question this system. It was the period of European migration and the beginning of global industrialization. Populations were growing more concentrated in urban areas as many began to work in the new industries or services, becoming part of an emerging middle class. This new middle class wanted to be heard and have their needs recognized, and the old system of power for a few no longer coincided with their interests. This development would lead to the slow weakening of oligarchic power and pave the way, in some countries, for a new political phenomenon known as "populism."

What is populism? In Latin America, it is a way to make policy based on charismatic leadership; a person who will serve as an intermediary between the parties. It is a political way in which the leader, governor, or president will talk directly to the people, presenting himself as a kind of redeemer or savior who will help all, with a paternalist and authoritarian behavior. In this sense, populist leaders often advocate adopting positions of nationalist opposition to foreign capital and old politicians.

Movements and populist regimes began to proliferate in Latin America beginning in 1930. In most cases populism and strong centralized governments were established under the direction of reformist leaders who were charismatic, authoritarian, and had great popular support. This happened in Brazil with Getúlio Vargas (1930–1945), in Argentina with Juan Domingo Perón (1946–1955), in Mexico with Lázaro Cárdenas (1934–1940), in Guatemala with Jacobo Arbenz (1950–1954), and in other countries as well.

In these countries the populist politicians, although authoritarian, made some improvements during this period. The populist governments invested in basic industries in order to provide raw materials and energy at low cost to the private sector. In Brazil, Vargas worked to raise wages and implement reforms favorable to workers, and introduced labor laws, most of which are still in place. In Argentina, Perón started social legislation. Social concern was also present in agrarian reforms instituted by Cárdenas in Mexico and Arbenz in Guatemala.

But as the government was based on a person, not in democratic representation, one of the effects of populism was the deterioration of institutions such as the parliament. As a result during the 1950s, the majority of the countries in Latin America found themselves without strong political and party structure and stable institutions that they could rely on during a severe crisis.

In Brazil, the Vargas government was overthrown in 1945, under pressure from civil society and broad sectors of the armed forces. In Argentina, Perón was deposed in 1955 by a military coup backed by the oligarchs. In Guatemala Jacobo Arbenz was removed after he attempted an agrarian reform by a military coup supported by CIA (1954). Of the four classic cases of populism during that period, only Cárdenas left the government after elections were held in 1940.

The Cuban Revolution

Cuba was a Spanish colony from the sixteenth century until 1898, when the country, inspired by the writer and revolutionary, José Martí, gained its independence from Spain. An organized rebel force that received help from the United States, which had major investments in Cuba, led the independence movement. In return, the United States demanded a number of concessions. One was the Platt Amendment, signed in 1901, which gave the United States the right to intervene in Cuba whenever US interests were threatened and also when there were threats to US military bases on the island.

In the first half of the twentieth century, Cuba was ruled mostly by corrupt and violent dictators. Under Fulgencio Batista, who was elected president from 1940 to 1944, and then through a coup became dictator from 1952 to 1959, much of the island's wealth was concentrated in the hands of a few local families and American businesses, including the North American crime syndicate, which exploited casinos and prostitution in Havana. Meanwhile, the majority of the Cuban population lived in poverty, suffering from a lack of health services, diseases, and illiteracy.

Denouncing this situation, the young lawyer Fidel Castro sought to depose the Batista regime through legal channels. When the court ignored his challenges he and his brother, Raúl, gathered a group of fighters and

Tomas Rivero casts a net as he fishes on the Pilcomayo River outside of Villamontes, Bolivia. This portion of the river is inside the protected Aguaragüe National Park and Integrated Management Natural Area. *(Paul Jeffrey)*

began an armed movement to overthrow the Batista dictatorship. After a failed attack on a military barracks, during which many in his group were killed, Fidel Castro was imprisoned for two years. Subsequently, he and his brother went into exile in Mexico where they met Argentine doctor Ernesto "Che" Guevara and planned the overthrow of the Batista government. They returned to Cuba and with various rebel groups began the guerrilla war against the government. After battling for two years, the rebels won some popular support. Multiple attempts by the government to crush the revolution ended in failure. Batista fled Cuba on January 1, 1959, and Fidel Castro took over.

Fidel Castro initiated many measures, including the redistribution of land and the nationalization of major US-owned companies, to fight corruption and social and economic inequities. The United States answered by breaking diplomatic relations with Cuba and boycotting Cuban sugar. These actions began a period of crisis between Cuba and the United States from which grew major repercussions. In 1961, a military force comprised of Cuban exiles—trained and funded by the US government—invaded Cuba's Bay of Pigs in an attempt to overthrow the Cuban anti-imperialist government. After three days of fighting, the invasion was defeated. Under pressure from the United States, the Organization of American States (OAS) suspended Cuba's membership in that body. Another important consequence of the tense relationship between Cuba and the United States was the economic embargo imposed on Cuba by the United States beginning in February 1962. At first, the embargo did not affect trade between Cuba and countries other than the United States, but since that time, the United States has pressured other nations and American companies with foreign subsidiaries to restrict trade with Cuba.[9]

Imperialism on the Scene

After World War II, there was a period when the elites in Latin America, dissatisfied with populism, decided to join foreign economic groups, especially from the United States in order to strengthen economic growth.

Thus, since 1950, there has been a massive influx of multinational companies in the region, taking advantage of not only the natural resources but also of the abundant and cheap workforce.

One example was the Alliance for Progress, announced by President John F. Kennedy at the Economic and Social Conference in Punta Del Este (Uruguay) in August 1961. Among other details, the conference tried to enhance some programs of agrarian reform in Latin America, to end illiteracy, and improve income distribution. This initiative was also an attempt to prevent the ideas of the Cuban Revolution from spreading across the continent and encouraging nationalist movements to adopt Marxists positions.[10]

One of the countries to closely monitor this process was Brazil. In 1948, under the presidency of General Eurico Gaspar Dutra, the country's government organized Escola Superior de Guerra (Superior School of War). It was inspired by the National War College in the United States, which was a center of studies and training of US military and civilian leaders.

During the 1960s and 1970s, the Alliance for Progress policy would lead to growing US intervention in the formation of the Latin American military elite. It also extended the US influence in Latin American politics to all the countries of the region. Besides a way of ensuring political power on the continent it was also part of a strategy to prevent the influence of communism from spreading to other countries in Latin America.

Although maintaining its profession of faith in democracy, the US government was a strong supporter of various dictatorships in Central America and the Caribbean, such as Rafael Trujillo in the Dominican Republic, Anastasio Somoza García in Nicaragua, and Fulgencio Batista in Cuba. Furthermore, in 1954, the United States supported the military coup that overthrew President Jacobo Arbenz of Guatemala who was responsible for putting in place nationalist measures that were favorable to the country's development. This kind of US support happened in other Latin American countries as well.

The Latin American Dictatorships and Democratization Process

In the 1960s, the fragile democracies of South America began to be replaced by military dictatorships set up by coups generally supported by the United States. The first of these occurred in Argentina with the overthrow of President Arturo Frondizi in 1962. Then it happened in Brazil, where President João Goulart, who had been legally elected and proposed nationalist and democratic reforms, was deposed on March 31, 1964, by a military coup backed by the United States. In the same year, President Víctor Paz Estenssoro, who had come to power in Bolivia by a popular revolution in 1952, was overthrown.

In 1973, the socialist president of Chile, Salvador Allende, who had been democratically elected, was killed during a bloody coup that brought to power General Augusto Pinochet. Also in 1973, President Juan María Bordaberry in Uruguay dissolved the General Assembly and installed a repressive dictatorial regime supported by the military. Three years later, Argentina was again convulsed by a military coup that deposed President Isabelita Isabel Perón, third wife of General Juan Domingo Perón, who had returned to power in 1973.

During this cycle of military dictatorships, political persecution, annulment of democratic rights, torture, and the disappearances and murders of opponents became common in the political life of the region.

It is necessary to point out how harsh the dictatorship governments were towards anyone who dared to combat, denounce, fight against, or just question the government. During this period which lasted from around 1960 to 1985, most Latin Americans lived strongly repressed lives and some of them were sentenced under military dictatorships that had cruel methods to suppress people's resistance.

This time of darkness was characterized by denial of freedom of expression, non-elected rulers, and political repression, left deep scars. According to the report of the Brazilian Secretariat for Human Rights, the number of prisoners being held was huge in the southern region of Latin America from 1960 to 1985. In Argentina, nearly 30,000 people were abducted. Under the Augusto Pinochet government, the number of disappeared in Chile varied from 3,000 to 10,000 people. In Brazil, the estimated number of people who were affected in some way by the dictatorship's repression was 50,000 people, including those who were killed, arrested, tortured, and exiled.[11]

Other countries also suffered setbacks through takeovers and subsequent implementation of dictatorial regimes. Assuming power a decade earlier in Paraguay, in 1954, the military dictatorship of General Alfredo Stroessner only began to weaken in 1989. François "Papa Doc" Duvalier was elected president of Haiti in 1957. His ascent to power was the beginning of a bloody dictatorship based on torture and terror. He remained in office until his death in 1971, and was succeeded by his son, "Baby Doc," who was overthrown by a popular uprising in 1986.

Despite all these conflicts and the lack of democracy in the region, the military elite in power opened the economy to foreign capital and implemented a development model based on the concentration of income and flattening of wages. In some countries, like Brazil, there was economic modernization during the military cycle. And as a result of the concessions made to the multinationals, foreign debt increased and inflation led to the collapse of this model, causing the economic crises in Latin America that began in the late 1970s.

The fact is that the economy in Latin America—marked by the growth of external debt—underpaid salaries and wages, led to the loss of purchasing power of much of the population, and together with unemployment increased social inequalities.

Politically, the most visible effect of the economic crisis was the strengthening of the democratic opposition that demanded a return to authoritarian rule of law. Gradually, opposition groups began to mobilize larger sectors of society, forcing the military governments to make concessions that led to the restoration of democratic normality in several countries. Between 1979 and 1990, thirteen countries returned to democratic rule, including Bolivia (1982), Argentina (1983), Uruguay (1984), Brazil (1985), Guatemala (1985), and Chile (1990).

Latin America Democracies and Old Problems

From the 1990s, the deep social inequality and the end of dictatorships in many countries in Latin America led to the election of left-leaning parties of different hues of government. The outcome of these elections was considered a new "red wave" in the area. A prime example is the election of Hugo Chávez in 1998 in Venezuela. Another election is that of Luiz Inácio Lula da Silva as president of Brazil in 2002. These elections revealed various attempts and proposals to address social inequality and economic problems. The seizure of power of these governments was also a reaction to questioning or open opposition to the consequences of globalization, privatization, deregulation of labor, and the actions of US interference—the most influential power in the region—as well as multilateral organizations such as the International Monetary Fund (IMF).

An improved outlook in Latin America occurred after decades of political turmoil and economic instability. Many of the Latin American countries in recent decades such as Brazil, Argentina, and Chile ended their eras of military dictatorship with a shift to democracy and freedom of politics. This led to a realization of free elections, the beginning of more democratic governments, and economic improvement on the continent.

We can say that this transition period started a new geo-political organization in the region, forming three groups of countries, more or less defined by

trends in their government: the Bolivarian bloc, the Moderate countries, and the Conservative countries.

The Nationalists—Bolivarian Bloc

This bloc, headed by Venezuela, consists of Cuba, Bolivia, Nicaragua, the Dominican Republic, Ecuador, Antigua and Barbuda, St. Lucia and St. Vincent and the Grenadines, leads policies that are more nationalistic, anti-liberal, and in open opposition to the United States.

Venezuela

Critical of what he called US imperialism, former Venezuelan President Hugo Chávez started illiberal policies in 2005, when it declared its adherence to what he called "socialism of the twenty-first century." Among his measures were broad agrarian reform processes, encouraging forms of co-management between state and workers, and the expansion of state control over strategic industries, especially in oil exploration, which is the main wealth of the country.

For Chávez, the Venezuelan Bolivarian Revolution was inspired by Simón Bolívar, hero of the independence of the country as well as several other Latin American nations that were formed in the nineteenth century. With the death of Chávez and the election of Nicolás Maduro, there is uncertainty about which direction the country will take, the continuity of "socialism of the twenty-first century" as the colonel liked to refer to government measures, is threatened, as well as various social assistance programs that were developed during the 14 years he headed the presidency.

Bolivia

In the poorest country in South America, the government of Evo Morales nationalized the oil and gas exploration in 2006, which was the central campaign issue of his election, supported by a broad popular movement that brought together unions, neighborhood associations, students, and associations of coca growers (a plant traditionally used in the country). Since then, relations between the US and Bolivia have been tense. Bolivia expelled the US ambassador in 2008, accusing him of

Weenhayek indigenous fishers pull in a net on the Pilcomayo River outside of Villamontes, Bolivia. The Weenhayek have had to struggle against large agricultural plantations and cattle raisers to retain access to the river. *(Paul Jeffrey)*

conspiring against the Bolivian government. In early 2013, relations worsened when the United States suspected that Edward Snowden, the former National Security Agency contractor accused of leaking secret information from the US government, was a passenger on Evo Morales' plane.

Ecuador

President Rafael Correa was reelected with 57 percent of the vote in February 2013, and managed to form a bench support with more than 50 percent in Congress. With this, he will be able to approve most of his electoral projects. Correa called an assembly, which approved a new constitution and nationalized industries, such as oil and gas.

The Moderates

Brazil, Argentina, Uruguay, and Peru form a group of countries with moderate leftist governments which adopt policies that combat poverty. Many of them had a recent democratic shift with elections and they are struggling to stabilize their economy with growth.

Argentina

President Cristina Fernández de Kirchner was reelected in 2011 mainly due to the economic growth of 9 percent per year and social inclusion programs. In 2012, she accused Repsol, a Spanish oil company, of underinvesting in Argentine oil firm YPF. As a consequence, the Argentine government expropriated the 51 percent of Repsol's stake, assumed the majority control of investment, and became the major stockholder in YPF. Another measure considered nationalistic was the approval of the Law on Media, which stipulates rules and limits to the media in the country. The government says it plans to eliminate monopolies, but suffers accusations of wanting to control the media and stifle criticism, especially of the Clarín Group, the country's largest media corporation. President Kirchner lost popularity in 2012 because of rising inflation, the reduction in GDP growth (estimated at 2 percent in 2012), and restrictions on buying dollars and imports.

The government also has been facing strikes by workers demanding increased wages.

Brazil

Many governments consider Brazil as the natural leader in Latin America. It is the continent's largest country and wields immense political and economic power. At the same time, Brazil has a history of peace, sharing borders with 10 countries without any diplomatic problems or conflicts with any of them in recent history. Furthermore, the country has acted as an intermediary in regional conflicts.

The country has had its first woman president, Dilma Rousseff, since January 2011. Her predecessor was the former union leader, Luiz Inácio Lula da Silva, whose government was known for its emphasis on fighting poverty. Lula worked toward improving economic inequality through the expansion of social programs like Bolsa Família, and the policy of increasing the minimum wage with increases above inflation. This brought to market masses of people who, until then, had been unable to acquire even basic items. During his governance, 20.5 million Brazilians who had been living on less than a quarter of the minimum wage per month were able to escape extreme poverty.

Peru

The former military officer Ollanta Humala, who was once declared a nationalist, is considered a Bolivarian and an ally of Hugo Chávez. He was elected president in 2011 on a platform of the moderate left. He keeps the liberal economic policies of his predecessor and, like former Brazilian president Lula, has adopted social programs and measures to encourage education. Peru is one of the countries in South America with a growing economy, the result of high international prices for minerals, and increase in domestic consumption, and a reduction of poverty.

The Conservatives

The US has allies in conservative governments, including Colombia's Juan Manuel Santos, Chile's

Sebastián Piñera, and more recently, Mexico's Enrique Peña Nieto.

Colombia

As the closest US ally in South America, Colombia maintains an agreement on free trade. In 2009, the United States announced the construction of military bases in "the country": military bases in the country to which US troops will have access. The official reason for this was to support Colombia in combating drug trafficking (Colombia is the world's largest producer of cocaine), as well as leftist guerrillas—the Revolutionary Armed Forces of Colombia (Fuerzas Armadas Revolucionarios de Colombia [FARC]) and National Liberation Army (Ejército de Liberación Nacional [ELN]).

After decades of conflict, recently some peace negotiations have started. In October 2012, FARC, weakened by military actions against them, announced a truce and agreed to peace negotiations with the Colombian authorities. The government rejected the truce, but agreed to the peace talks. In January 2013, the conflict resumed but the dialogue continues. In early 2013, the guerrilla group ELN officially requested their inclusion in peace negotiations.

Mexico

Among Latin American countries, Mexico has the most intimate relationship with the United States. The Mexican economy became officially linked to the economy of its northern neighbors when it signed the North American Free Trade Agreement (NAFTA) in 1994. The deal, engineered to reduce or eliminate trade tariffs between the United States, Canada, and Mexico, has allowed US industries, attracted by tax subsidies and cheap labor, to install themselves in Mexico. NAFTA, however, left the Mexican economy highly dependent on the US economy. Mexico is the third-largest supplier of oil to its neighbor in the north.

Former Mexican President Felipe Calderón, who stepped down in December 2012, was a major US ally. The current president, Enrique Peña Nieto, although in opposition to Calderón, has indicated that Mexico will remain in close liaison with the United States.

Drug trafficking and organized crime are the biggest problems faced by Mexico today. The violence caused by the dispute between criminal groups is particularly prevalent in the northern region of the country. Analysts estimate that the dismantling of drug cartels in Colombia in the 1990s caused much of the drug activity to relocate to the Mexican territory. The Mexican government has been waging an offensive against traffickers since 2006, with military and police reinforcement in critical areas.

Chile

In 2003, then-president Ricardo Lagos signed the United States-Chile Free Trade Agreement. Since ratification, presidents Sebastián Piñera (2010-2014) and Michelle Bachelet (2006-2010; 2014-present) have championed Chile's economic growth resulting from the bilateral agreement. President Bachelet currently faces challenges from students and the general public regarding the country's public education system, especially secondary and higher education levels.

Paraguay

The nation was also aligned with the moderate group during the government of President Fernando Lugo, who was impeached in June 2012 after four years in office. His departure caused the suspension of the participation of Paraguay in Mercosur, the Southern Common Market, which is an economic alliance among Argentina, Brazil, Paraguay, Uruguay, Venezuela, and Bolivia. Vice President Federico Franco assumed power until the elections in April 2013, when Horacio Cartes, an important local businessman from the Colorado Party with conservative tendencies, was elected.

Recent Waves of Immigrants

After the influx of European immigrants seeking better living conditions the Americas that began in the second half of the nineteenth century and continued into the beginning of the twentieth century, there was a change in migration. From 1960 until the beginning of the twentieth-first century people were emigrating from developing countries to the developed countries and economies of the Northern Hemisphere.

Peoples left their lands seeking higher incomes, better social services and opportunities, as well as to avoid social and political conflicts, human rights violations, and natural disasters. According to the UN-Habitat report, it is estimated that in 2010 more than 30 million people from Latin America and the Caribbean (5.2 percent) lived outside their country of origin, with the preferred countries being the United States, Canada, and Spain.[12]

Until recently, most of the developed countries usually facilitated the entry of specialized labor and tolerated underpaid skilled labor. Over time, with the international economic crisis, the rich nations have established stricter laws, and in some situations, built walls and fences to prevent migration. This is the case of the US border with Mexico. In 2006 President George W. Bush signed the Secure Fence Act and initiated building a 3,200-kilometer (1,988-mile) wall along the US-Mexico border.

Mexico is highlighted as the country with the largest number of migrants in the world (nearly 12 million Mexicans live abroad, equivalent to 10.7 percent of its population), and for being a place of transit for immigrants from other countries traveling on to the United States. After Mexico, the countries in the region with the largest number of emigrants are Colombia, Brazil, El Salvador, Cuba, Ecuador, Peru, Dominican Republic, Haiti, and Jamaica.

The situation in Brazil is somewhat different with only 0.4 percent of the population as emigrant and their main destinations the United States, Spain, and Japan (due to the large number of people in Brazil who are of Japanese descent).

Another kind of immigration is the movement within Latin America. This kind of internal migration is based on geographical, historical, and cultural proximity, including the support that many find and the common language, Spanish, that is spoken in most of countries of Latin America. There are also some movements of people who left their land of origin motivated by economic or political issues. For example, the political violence of the 1970s and 1980s in El Salvador, Guatemala, and Nicaragua caused people from those countries to migrate to Belize and Costa Rica, Antigua and Barbuda, and Grenada.

Besides political causes and economic conditions, the consequences of natural disasters have also become factors in migration. In this case, it is important to mention Haiti, one of the poorest countries in the hemisphere, which was devastated by an earthquake in 2010 that led many families to look for a better place to live and work. Sixty-four percent of all foreigners in the Dominican Republic come from Haiti. At the same time, 10 percent of the Dominican population has immigrated to other countries, mainly the United States.

Haitian refugees have also been moving to other countries in Latin America, such as the northern region of Brazil. As the number of Haitian immigrants has been increasing enormously, the Brazilian government has issued a quota of visas and is applying some restrictions. Haitians also are going to Peru, Ecuador, Colombia, and other nearby countries in their search for better living. In Chapter 5, we will see how United Methodist Women has been supporting partners in Haiti for many years and is also involved in the long-term recovery efforts of Haiti to rebuild their lives and livelihoods in the aftermath of the January 2010 earthquake.

Brazil, with its recent economic growth, has become a newly desired destination for people in many countries, including Europeans. They are mainly from those countries facing economic challenges and employment crises such as Spain and Portugal. Also, the lack of a qualified workforce in Brazil has attracted skilled workers from many countries and at the same time is a reason many Brazilians who lived abroad are returning to their country.

Pedro Canales harvests food in Honduras from a small plot of land overlooking the Gulf of Fonseca. Along with other families in his village, he has lost access to some land and parts of the ocean in recent years as the wealthiest family in Honduras has moved in and fenced off vast areas. *(Paul Jeffrey)*

Profiles

Célia and Pepe

This is a story told by two people. That they complete each other is the fruit of a partnership that has lasted more than three decades. Having two daughters, who are 23 and 25 years old, Célia and Pepe have a peaceful life. "I am living the best time of my life. I can wake up later, do things in my time," says Célia, who spent many years of her life working part-time to be able to take her daughters to school, to English classes, and other activities.

Célia worked as a librarian at Universidade de São Paulo (USP), a public university in São Paulo, for more than 20 years. When she retired, she was invited to organize a library for a non-governmental organization in São Paulo. "Everything was piled inside, and the door was always closed." Now the material is all centralized and at hand for all of the professionals. "People started to like using the library, and I began to subscribe to magazines which have more updated information." Célia is proud of what she does. "I like my job very much. I even like Mondays. If someone asks me about a book we don't have in the library, I don't just say we don't have it. I research and tell them where to find it." On weekends, she organizes private libraries. But working in libraries wasn't her first plan; she originally wanted to be a teacher. She even taught in public schools, but was disappointed with the teaching system being so closed: "We learn such beautiful things that we can't put into practice... but I refused to engage in the scheme."

In the 1980s, Pepe, who is Peruvian, came to Brazil to study in the university. He arrived by himself and, in the beginning, he was shocked by the size of São Paulo. He also found the food strange. Lima is a coastal city where people are very used to eating fish and a variety of dishes. "Here, people eat too much meat, and have rice and beans every day." He also missed his family, but soon he made friends from other cities and states in Brazil, and they made up a kind of family.

Célia and Pepe met at the university in the 1980s, and they like to tell stories from that time: all of the students in the university housing were thrown out during the period of dictatorship, but they both participated in a group of students that pressured the university so that the place could be used by students again. They even participated in an invasion and then went to live there. That period was very important, and made different lessons and experiences possible: "We lived with students from several countries. There was a community TV room and a kitchen. Everybody cooked and brought food to eat together. We got to know food from many countries. At the parties, we used to dance Greek, Indian dances . . . There were students from different cultures that lived together easily."

What's their entertainment? "Every Friday, we buy some wine, cheese, and pastes, and stay at home." They also like to dance, but they haven't done it much lately. When they were university students, they used to go to a lot of parties: "In Peru, parties are basically made to dance," Célia says. "He has always danced very well. And, with him, I learned how to dance salsa, merengue."

Célia is a "Spiritist," a Christian doctrine started in the nineteenth century by the French educator Allan Kardec. The Spiritists believe in reincarnation, in the possibility of communication between living and dead people.[13] Since she was very young, Célia was curious about Spiritism, and she went to take courses. She goes to a Spiritist center weekly. Pepe is not religious, although he was baptized and grew up in a Catholic family. "We got married in a Catholic church in Peru because they think the blessing is very important," Célia says. "The girls were baptized, took Communion, and attended those catechism classes. I thought it was important to them to know all of that." Nowadays, they go to the Spiritist center, too. On the other hand, Pepe says he is "very rational," but he respects and attentively listens to his wife's point of view.

Fabiana Hiromi

A smell of fresh sushi, children playing in the backyard and around the house, and the same old picture: all of the cousins sitting on the stairs. Those are some of Fabiana's childhood memories. Her grandma's home was where she and her cousins used to meet, in the suburbs of São Paulo. Her grandparents were Japanese and came to Brazil in the 1950s when they were almost grown-ups. Today she is a journalist and works in a non-governmental organization where she is a website editor and writes about public policies and education.

Fabiana lives in São Paulo with Fábio, her husband for two-and-a-half years now. They met at work while she was at the university. When they want to have fun, they like going to the cinema and concerts. This year, the couple traveled to New York for one week. Fabiana thinks the city is amazing for its diversity and dynamism: "There are thousands of things you can do. Everything was like scenes in a movie: people sitting on the stairs, some guys smoking in the streets." She also acknowledges the great inequalities in the city.

Some years ago, she went through a difficult situation in her family: her mother's death due to bowel cancer. "In situations like that, the whole family gets sick." What gave her strength? "I'm not religious. I was baptized, studied in a Catholic school, but I didn't take Communion. My mother followed Seicho-No-Ie (a religion of Japanese origins with Buddhist inspiration), which teaches gratitude and the acceptance of problems and challenges in life. In situations like that, people usually get more spiritualized, but it made me question more. She had such a strong faith and suffered so much. I thought that was a little unfair." In spite of that, Fabiana believes it's necessary to keep in touch with her own spirituality.

(Paul Jeffrey)

Elsa Juarez, a Wichí indigenous woman in Santa Victoria Este, Argentina, tightens the strap on her broom before sweeping the ground around her home. *(Paul Jeffrey)*

Endnotes

1. Lucia Lippi Oliveira, *O Brasil dos Imigrantes* (Rio de Janeiro: Jorge Zahar Editor, 2001), 23–24.

2. Noemí Acreche and María Virginia Albeza, "El siglo de las migraciones: entre el pluralismo y la fusión," *Exposía*, accessed October 20, 2014, www.expoesia.com/media/Ponencia_Acreche%20y%20Albeza.pdf.

3. Ed Cottrell, "Growth and Development of Protestantism in Latin America," *Religious Studies 282: Introduction to Christianity*, last modified May 13, 2000, www.edcottrell.com/downloads/protestantisminlatinamerica.pdf.

4. Ricardo, "History of Protestantism in South America from 1492 to 1901," *A Post-Modern Protestant in Paris* (blog), last modified January 7, 2009, protestant-in-paris.blogspot.com.br/2009/01/history-of-protestantism-in-south.html.

5. "Historico metodismo no Brasil," *Igreja Metodista Portal Nacional*, last modified September 14, 2013, www.metodista.org.br/historico-metodismo-no-brasil.

6. Pablo Deiros, *Protestantismo en America Latina* (Grupo Nelson, 1997), 26.

7. Rui de Souza Josgrilberg, "A Autonomia e a cultura brasileira," *Revista Caminhando*, v. 10, n. 2 (2005), www.metodista.br/revistas/revistas-ims/index.php/CA/article/viewArticle/1274.

8. Antonio Gouveia Mendonça, "O Protestantismo no Brasil e suas Encruzilhadas," *Revista USP* (São Paulo: setembro/novembro, 2005), 48–67.

9. Rainer Gonçalves Sousa, "Revolução Cubana," *Mundo Educação*, accessed October 20, 2014, www.mundo-educacao.com/historia-america/revolucao-cubana.htm.

10. "Alliance for Progress (*Alianza para el Progreso*)" John F. Kennedy Presidential Library and Museum, accessed June 10, 2013, www.jfklibrary.org/JFK/JFK-in-History/Alliance-for-Progress.aspx.

11. "Direito à verdade e à memória: Comissão Especial sobre Mortos e Desaparecidos Políticos," (Brasília: Secretaria Especial dos Direitos Humanos, 2007), www.sdh.gov.br/assuntos/mortos-e-desaparecidos-politicos/pdfs/livro-direito-a-memoria-e-a-verdade.

12 "The State of Latin American and Caribbean Cities 2012," UN-Habitat, August 2012, www.unhabitat.org/pmss/listItemDetails.aspx?publicationID=3386.

13. Allan Kardec, "The Spiritist Doctrone, Codefied," the *Spiritist Psychological Society*, accessed October 20, 2014, www.spiritistps.org/en/the-spiritist-doctrine.

Eight-year-old Vanesa Silva de Soza in the rain in the Esperança Sustainable Development Project, where Sister Dorothy Stang, a U.S. nun, was murdered for her defense of the forest and the landless poor. *(Paul Jeffrey)*

Chapter 3

Confronting Historical Problems: Toward Equality

The previous chapters presented a brief historical perspective of Latin America: the wide variety of people, colonization struggles, the different paths to independence, and recent events. It is important to consider that the Latin American reality is tied to a larger scenario, which involves other countries in the world and the region's role in the world economy. In many cases Latin American countries are subordinated to the stronger economies of the Northern Hemisphere, such as the United States and many European countries. At the same time the region is still developing and growing in its importance and participation in the global economy, which allows it to participate in The International Forum—recognizing not only Latin America's economic achievements, but also its cultural relevance.

This chapter will turn to present the challenges in the lives of Latin Americans, their daily struggle owing to lack of housing and food, while facing racism, violence against women, exploitation of children, and more. It is important to point out that the living conditions in Latin America can vary greatly among countries and social status. For example, the life of a college student in Haiti, a country devastated by the earthquake of 2010, could be quite different from a college student in Chile, which has higher indices of literacy and income, and is considered more industrialized. At the same time, the daily life in rural areas differs from life in urban areas.

This chapter, therefore, attempts to present the main issues that the region faces related to education, health, domestic violence, child labor, and concerns regarding race that confront blacks and indigenous people in the region. Nevertheless, it is important to point out that many of the problems in Latin America such as racism and violence against women are not exclusive to the region or originated there, but are widespread around the world and demand comprehensive understanding and action in order to overcome them wherever they occur.

Despite its problems, however, Latin America is currently experiencing a favorable period of economic growth. After two decades with many of its countries experiencing low rates of development and serious economic crises in the 1980s and 1990s, the growth of economic activity in Latin America beginning in the 2000s has resulted in increased employment and tax revenue, which allows the governments to invest in improvements and combat old problems.

The living conditions are improving in almost all countries in the region—from Mexico in the north to Argentina and Chile in the south. Among the key factors that have enabled this economic growth is the increase in the international prices of raw materials (the main item on the balance for exports from the region), expansion of foreign investments, economic and political stability, and the shift to more democratic governments in most countries in the region.

Although most Latin American countries are not yet part of the most powerful group in the global economy, they are working to be current with technological advances so they can incorporate them into their industries and production processes.

The main center of economic decisions still is based in countries of the Northern Hemisphere, such as the

United States and Europe. They tend to influence or make decisions for many of the world's nations. However, some Latin America countries, including Brazil, Mexico, and Argentina, are managing in different ways and are beginning to be directly involved with global decision maker groups, such as the G-20 (a group of 20 major economies in the world consisting of 19 countries plus the European Union).

Within this scenario, there are some policies and programs in place to fight poverty in order to increase the development of nations and overcome historical problems. Moderate or left wing governments have initiated many of these programs, which have made combatting inequality a priority. Latin America is the region with the greatest inequality in the world, which means that there is a lot of wealth concentrated in small portions of the population, while large numbers of people live in poverty under miserable conditions.

What Is Inequality?

It is said that a country is unequal when there are uneven opportunities and rewards offered to different segments of the population based on social, economic, and ethnic status. These inequalities are socially built in many ways and vary according to country, society, or community, but they are all influenced by history, culture, geography, and religion. At the same time, the inequality is visible also in a systemic and structured pattern of the distribution of wealth, opportunities, education, health care, access to goods, rewards, and punishments.

We can say that access to quality public services, including education, nutrition, and health care is not available to all populations due to lack of infrastructure and capable professionals. Also, because public services are concentrated in urban areas they are not accessible to rural populations. High quality public services are then reserved for a small percentage of the population that can pay for those services and afford to live where they are offered.

The inequality in access to education generates a vicious circle. The children of those who can afford to pay for a better education are best educated, and obviously can get the best jobs. Meanwhile, the poor end up with minimal or low-quality education, which diminishes their chances for social mobility.

A study conducted by the World Bank in 2003 shows that the countries with the highest index of inequality in Latin America are Guatemala, followed by Honduras, Colombia, and Brazil, and the countries on the lower index of inequality are Costa Rica, Ecuador, El Salvador, Peru, Uruguay, and Venezuela.[1]

Where gender, race, and ethnicity are determinants for job opportunities, health care, and education, inequality prevails. Indigenous and Afro-descendant people are at a considerable disadvantage compared to white people, who receive the highest wages in the region, and have more years of schooling. The study also shows that indigenous men in Brazil, Guyana, Guatemala, Bolivia, Chile, Mexico, and Peru earn 35–65 percent less than white men. The disparity in wages between white women and non-white women was in the same range. In Brazil, men and women of African descent earn about 50 percent less than their white counterparts.[2]

In countries such as Guatemala, Bolivia, and Brazil, where the percentage of ethnic and non-white people is significant, more than 50 percent of households headed by white men or women have access to sewage facilities as compared to 30 percent of those headed by indigenous men or women. "Across the region, citizens who are both female and of indigenous or African descent are at the bottom of all asset-distribution scales."[3]

In contrast to enduring gaps related to racial and ethnic differences, Latin America has experienced progress in narrowing gender differentials in education. In much of the region, girls and young women are actually overtaking boys and young men in educational attainment.[4]

Regarding education access, even though public systems exist in most countries there are many differences in terms of social classes. In Mexico, the average person in the poorer sectors of the population has 3.5 years of schooling, as compared to 11.6 years for the average person in the wealthier sectors.[5] In many countries, educational attainment also differs among ethnic and racial groups; gender inequality, though improving, still exists.

The same research shows that health outcomes also vary dramatically along with income distribution, resulting in enormous impacts on quality of life and opportunities. In Brazil, children born to households of the poorest parts the population are three times as likely to die before they reach the age of five compared to children born to prosperous households; in Bolivia this figure is more than four times as high.

Fighting Poverty

With the recent waves of stability and economic development in Latin America, there are fewer people in extreme poverty. In 1990, 48.4 percent of all Latin Americans were poor or extremely poor, totaling 215 million people. According to the World Bank, a person is considered poor when they live on less than $1.25 to $2.50 per day. In 2011, this proportion decreased to 29.4 percent, but as there was an increase in population during this period, there are still 168 million people in poverty, 100 million of whom are indigent.[6]

This improvement is a result of an increase in employment and income distribution programs such as Bolsa Família (Family Bag) in Brazil, which is directed towards families that are considered to be living in poverty and extreme poverty. There are some requirements for participants who receive this aid:
- Pregnant women in the family must go to periodical medical visits.
- Mothers have to attend education orientation for breastfeeding and healthy nutrition.
- Mothers must keep their children's vaccinations up-to-date.
- Children must have regular school attendance.

- Parents must participate in adult literacy programs, if necessary.

Programs similar to Bolsa Família have been extended in the region and are helping people in their struggle to overcome poverty. A 2012 survey conducted by the World Bank about poverty in Latin America found that from 2003 to 2009, over 49 million people rose above the poverty line, increasing the level of their average income to between 10 and 40 dollars per person a day. About 40 percent of this population was Brazilian, and there were also significant improvements in Mexico and Colombia.[7]

Living conditions in the region, however, vary widely. Countries such as Argentina, Chile, and Uruguay have low national poverty levels (less than 12 percent of the population), in contrast to Guatemala, Nicaragua, and Paraguay, where more than half the people are poor, and Honduras, where the poverty rate exceeds 60 percent. The most dramatic case is Haiti where poverty has increased to over 70 percent of the population following the 2010 earthquake. In absolute terms, of the approximately 124 million poor people in the region's cities, more than half live either in Brazil (37 million) or Mexico (25 million).[8]

But, why are so many people living in these conditions? There are multiple causes of such unequal societies, but they are all related to the past models of colonization—the enormous gap between the colonist exporters who settled in the rural areas and exploited the land and labor through slavery, the poorly compensated working population, and an economy that struggles to compete and develop to be part of the international market.

How Women Are More Affected by Inequalities

Although the inequalities in Latin America affect both men and women, statistics show that poverty affects women in many more ways and on a larger scale. However, it is important to point out how women have proven that they can accomplish and achieve much.

Millions of families have moved out of poverty through the work of women. Women have also had a crucial role in shaping the development of the region in the last decade. Without the incidence of women joining the workforce, extreme poverty in the region in 2010 would have been 30 percent higher. Nevertheless, women's participation in the labor force is linked to traditional women's occupations such as health care, beauty, and domestic services. These types of jobs are not only underpaid, but are also marked by instability and poor working conditions.

While there has been some progress in women's participation in the workforce, there are still wide gaps between men and women, which are far from closing, especially in terms of wages. In Chile, Brazil, Mexico, and Peru, professional men can expect to earn up to 25 percent more than their female colleagues in the same position.[9]

Domestic Violence

Another injustice that women in Latin America experience is the high rate of domestic violence, which is one of the primary causes of injury among women in the region. Worldwide, one in three women are victims of violence, but in some parts of Latin America the most recent figures place the number at one in every two.[10] The urgent need to overcome these tragic figures and the progress made in this area differs greatly from country to country.

Brazil has taken some initiatives to eradicate this type of violence by improving infrastructure and adopting innovative laws to address violence in the home, such as the adoption of the Maria da Penha Law that imposes more severe penalties on those who commit violence against women. This law is named as a tribute to Maria da Penha Maia Fernandes, a woman who suffered repeated aggression from her husband and even murder attempts that resulted in irreversible injuries to her health, such as paraplegia and other complications. However, Maria da Penha turned her pain into struggle, and became an example of solidarity and

the fight to overcome violence against women. With this initiative, the country experienced a 78 percent increase in the number of police stations and courts specialized in gender and domestic violence. Despite this, the prevalence of domestic violence in the country remains high with a 29 percent rate of women reporting abuse.

Childhood Scars

Forced labor of children in the region is another facet of inequality and discrimination in Latin America, especially against indigenous peoples. In 2009, a country mission of the United Nations Permanent Forum on Indigenous Issues (UNPFII) in Bolivia found evidence of sexual abuse of Guarani girls who worked in homes of landowners. In Ecuador, an assessment done by the ILO (International Labor Organization) of child labor in agriculture and domestic service found sexual exploitation widespread among both indigenous and non-indigenous groups. This kind of violation of the rights of girls and adolescents reveals the practice of property-style labor relations which allows the employer to "adopt" one or more children and assume upbringing and educational responsibilities for them while offering employment, which not always happens, because the children usually are working instead of studying, and sometimes don't even earn a salary. Some girls who do domestic work in household settings are between the ages of 6 and 12 years old.[11]

Bolivia National Statistics Institute and the ILO find that the ratio of indigenous children and adolescents participating in employment is far higher than their non-indigenous counterparts in both urban and rural areas.[12]

In Guatemala, an estimated 65 percent of domestic workers are indigenous girls and adolescents. Impoverished families often send their young female members to be employed as domestic laborers in towns and cities, where they work an average of 14 hours per day and are often at the risk of physical abuse, psychological abuse, and sexual harassment by employers and their

Rose Michel, a ten-year-old survivor of the January 12, 2010 earthquake in Haiti, lost both her legs when the orphanage she was living in collapsed. Here, she gets a hug from Maura Senfre, a volunteer from the Dominican-Haitian Women's Movement (MUDHA). *(Paul Jeffrey)*

family members. This situation is worsened by the lack of adequate remuneration and social security.

During the recent period of social, economic, and political transition following over three decades of armed conflict, indigenous girls and women in Guatemala were victims of various forms of violence. The Commission for Historical Clarification from Guatemala finds that 88 percent of those affected were Mayan women and girls who were systematically targeted for gender-based violence, particularly femicide in which indigenous women are murdered because they are women. Indigenous women are killed at a rate that is twice that of men. Rape has also been part of the counter-insurgency strategy. In 2011, 700 occurrences of femicide alone were reported to the Presidential Commission on Femicide. Bodies of victims were found to show signs of mutilation and sexual violence and were dumped in public areas, creating fear and insecurity within those communities.[13]

While most indigenous girls and young women in Guatemala were born following the conflict, they continue to live its legacy. A general climate of impunity and new forms of violence such as organized crime and criminal gangs perpetuate a tolerance of violence, which discourages victims from seeking protection and redress from the violence they suffered.[14]

Indigenous Peoples in Latin America
According to the International Work Group for Indigenous Affairs (IWGIA), it is estimated that there are 40,000,000 people in Latin America and the Caribbean who belong to the almost 600 different indigenous people group in the region, many of whom are in Mexico, Peru, Guatemala, Bolivia, and Ecuador. According to World Bank figures, 12.7 percent of the entire American population is indigenous.[15]

Each of these indigenous groups has their own culture, language, beliefs, and social organization, making each one of them unique; generalizations, therefore, should be avoided. Nevertheless, there are some characteristics that distinguish them in their position as indigenous peoples and they are confronted with common problems and challenges.

Despite being historically and culturally attached to their traditional territories located in rural areas, an increasing proportion of the indigenous population has become urban or dependent on urban clusters for their livelihood. At the same time, many indigenous families still have members in their communities of origin, but live in the cities and maintain ties with both realities. Ever since the period of colonization, more and more indigenous people migrated or have been displaced to regions or countries more or less distant from their communities of origin, and their connection with the land and community has been lost. These living conditions have a strong impact in sustaining the unique indigenous identity of the adults and of their children.

Extraction of Natural Resources in Indigenous Lands
Latin America is known for its vast natural resources and fertile land. This is also true of the land of indigenous people, but their struggle to keep their land has been limited and puts them at a disadvantage. There is growing competition between the governments of the region to attract new investments—the subsoil resources or biodiversity, the extractives and the export of raw materials, and the re-emergence of large agro-industrial estates are among the main attractions for investors.

At the same time, it's important to point out that indigenous peoples also face, in many cases, the inability and weaknesses of the government institutions to monitor and control the social and environmental effects of mining and agricultural development. In some situations this is due to a persistent racism that is manifested in the decision-makers' neglect of the rights of indigenous people and the protection of their land. It has led to a new level of inequity and conflict and a progressive impoverishment of the indigenous population. There is a lack of research about social and environmental impact before initiating large-scale projects, which leads great conflicts and disturbances in indigenous areas.

The IWGIA also notes that ecotourism can be defined as:

> New intergovernmental trade agreements with the economic powers of the developed world facilitate the dispossession of indigenous land and resources or their exploitation carried out without consultation and in exclusion of the indigenous inhabitants. The increasing investment capacity of national governments and businesses after a decade of sustained economic growth is directed towards the economic control of vast areas traditionally owned by indigenous peoples. The current degraded state of many indigenous territories, which are subject to large-scale extractive projects or have been stripped by mega road, port or hydroelectric power projects, affects indigenous peoples' fundamental rights to health, food and access to clean water.[16]

Gender and Indigenous Women

Indigenous women often face double discrimination. They are discriminated against as indigenous persons and as women. They experience discrimination, not only from the outside world, but also from within their own communities. Integration into society and the adoption of elements and behaviors of mainstream culture often leads to a further weakening of the status of women in indigenous societies.

Indigenous women thus suffer from a range of problems related to the violation of their rights. These include among others: lack of participation in decision-making processes, lack of control over income to sustain themselves and their families, lack of land rights, lack of access to education, domestic violence, and gender-based violence in situations of armed conflicts and militarization.

Racial and Ethnic Inequalities

The presence of Afro-descendant populations in Latin America varies greatly according to the country. In some countries in the Caribbean such as Jamaica, Saint Kitts and Nevis, Dominica, Saint Lucia, Haiti, Grenada, Guadeloupe, Barbados, Antigua and Barbuda, Saint Vincent and the Grenadines, the Bahamas, and the Dominican Republic, the black population exceeds 80 percent of the total population. The country with the largest number of Afro-descendants in the South American continent is Brazil with, according to the last census, an estimated 51 percent of the total population, which is equivalent to half the black population in the continent, about 100 million people.[17]

In most cases ethnicity in Latin America is defined based on physical characteristics like the kind of hair, shape of lips, or the skin color. Recent censuses have started to ask questions about whether people self-identify as indigenous or Afro-descendants.

South America is a region where large indices of miscegenation (racial mixing) have taken place, and many people, in an attempt to cover the existent racism, say that there is a harmonious coexistence between different peoples of the continent. Yet, it is still evident how the continent fosters social hierarchies that maintain a continuum of color perceptions, in which the lighter the skin color, the more white a person is, the more likely it is that he or she will be at the top of the social hierarchy. As the skin gets darker, the person is closer to the lower part in the social strata.

In Brazil, the miscegenation was somewhat flexible and widespread, making it somehow pliable for a racial classification. Brazilians are classified by color (white, black, brown, and yellow) and not by ethnicity. This attitude is also related to the belief in whitening or *embranquecimento*, as discussed in Chapter 2, where European immigration is explained. This belief was predominant in the late nineteenth century. The Brazilian elite, who were concerned about the large black population and believed this fact could lower the status of the country, decided to reduce the differences between blacks and whites by encouraging European immigration and intermarriage with black people with the purpose of producing children with lighter skin.

For Gilberto Freyre, a Brazilian anthropologist from the early twentieth century, miscegenation, was interpreted as something positive. The author states that the formation of Brazilian society is based on black, white, and indigenous peoples, which decisively influenced Brazilian culture, whether in its food habits, hygiene, or way of speaking.

Another concept of miscegenation is called the myth of "racial democracy." According to this concept, Brazil would be considered a land where the mixture of races generated a people without prejudice. However, this does not hold true. Black and indigenous people suffer daily from racism and discrimination in education and health care, and at work with inferior wages, as well from increased violence, and even discrimination in social relations.

Even today, with a growing influence of black and indigenous movements, there are countless episodes of violence, discrimination, and prejudice based on race and ethnicity conducted either by the police, or by the employers who avoid hiring an individual because of his or her skin color. Often violent and prejudiced attitudes are experienced in school and community as well.

It is important to understand that the inequalities imposed on the black and indigenous populations are the result of a process related to colonization that was based on the exploitation of land and labor through slavery. This situation continued in various ways even after the end of slavery because the former slaves were left without the necessary support for their development and were simply replaced by European immigrants who were given their jobs. Besides, there were so many problems within the social structure, such as difficulty in accessing quality health care and education, and few job opportunities in the labor market,

that part of the populavhgtion became conditioned to subordinate positions.

In this sense, social structures have helped to keep the majority of the individuals in vulnerable situations, in poverty, hunger, violence, and sickness. Although in general, the issues and struggles of people from Afro-descendants are similar to those of indigenous people, it is important to add that indigenous people additionally suffer from issues related to land demarcation and disrespect of their traditional knowledge and culture.

Countries like Brazil and Colombia are basing their affirmative action on conforming with the census figures. It happened also in Bolivia, in 2005, when President Evo Morales, assumed his indigenous identity (Aymara). Influenced by these changes, social movements are growing for Afro-descendants and indigenous people.

Although there are some recent changes related to racism that have been influenced by affirmative action, economic development and initiatives from social movements, most entrepreneurs, industry owners, TV stars, presenters, top politicians, and those with prestigious careers still tend to be more white.[18]

At the same time, the rate of infant mortality in most countries is higher for Afro-descendants and indigenous people. In Peru infant mortality rate among non-whites is 93 per 1,000 live births, compared to the white population, 45 per 1,000 live births. Similar ratios have been reported among black people in Colombia and Brazil. Afro-Latin Americans are over-represented among street children, homeless, prisoners, and less educated in most of countries.[19]

Women of African descent face significant challenges of violence, including sexual violence, and access to jobs and education. National media and tourist industries continue to present limiting and one-dimensional stereotypical and sexualized images of black women in places such as Bahia, Brazil, and Havana, Cuba. Meanwhile, many single black mothers face the daunting task of raising their children alone in underpaid jobs, like domestic work.[20]

Youth Mortality

Youth deaths, which are caused by violence, are a big issue in Latin America. A recent study by the World Health Organization (WHO) compiled by the Brazilian Center for Latin American Studies (CEBELA–Centro Brasileiro de Estudos Latino-Americanos) shows that El Salvador and Honduras lead in youth homicides, followed by the Virgin Islands, Trinidad and Tobago, Venezuela, Colombia, Guatemala, Brazil, Panama, Puerto Rico, and the Bahamas. For every 100,000 inhabitants in Brazil, 27.4 are victims of crimes. In the case of young people between 14 and 25 years old, the index rises to 54.8.[21]

According to this study, these rates are explained by the impact of structural problems related to political, economic, and social aspects, such as inequality and lack of access to basic services, combined with armed conflicts, including those that occurred in Guatemala, El Salvador, and Venezuela.

Data collected by the University of São Paulo in Brazil were also alarming. In the year 1995 the homicide rate in Brazil reached 23.83/100,000 inhabitants, while in the United States the figure remained at 8.22. The urban areas in Brazil had the worst homicide rates in the country. In 1997, the data showed 65.79 (Rio de Janeiro, state capital) and 56.69 (in São Paulo, state capital). The rates are even higher in neighborhoods with the most precarious living conditions, such as Jardim Angela, a neighborhood in the south of the city of São Paulo, which had a rate of 111.52 in 1995. Rates of this order are comparable to the cities that are undergoing or have had civil war or drug wars such as Bogota, Colombia.[22]

A recent study of Faculdade Latino-Americana de Ciências Sociais (FLACSO) and CEBELA points out that the incidents of deaths among the youth in Brazil is more than 500 times greater than that of Hong Kong, 273 times greater than that of Japan and England, and 137 times greater than that of Germany and Austria. Julio Jacobo Waiselfisz explained that violence has multiple causes and consequences. He points to three of the main causes—first is the culture of violence. According to Waiselfisz, in Latin America there is the custom of resolving conflicts with death, part of the legacy of the slave riders in the continent. Secondly, he points to the availability of firearms, mostly illegal arms. And the third cause is impunity or immunity from the law.[23]

A Rich Land for Its People

Eduardo Galeano is the Uruguayan writer known for his book titled *Open Veins of Latin America: Five Centuries of the Pillage of a Continent*. He is a keen critic of Latin American exploitation and inequalities. For Galeano, "our region still functions as a menial subordinate. It continues to exist servicing others' needs, as a source and reserve of oil and iron, of copper, beef, fruit and coffee. The raw materials and food destined for richer consuming countries that profit more from their consuming them rather than Latin America from producing them. The taxes collected by the buyers are much higher than the prices received by the sellers." Galeano's book provides a passionate view of how Latin America suffers, in many ways, from "the resource curse," where the vast amount of natural resources for many countries is more a source of problems than benefits in places of low and mid-income levels of development, especially for the developing countries.[24]

Latin America, including the Caribbean, is a land that has attracted and continues to attract greedy trespassers. Since colonial times their wealth in minerals, gold, silver, iron, lithium, and others resources such as oil, and the products of their fertile lands have been destined for outsiders rather than for their own people. The region has 65 percent of the world's reserves of lithium, as well as 42 percent of silver, 38 percent of copper, 33 percent of tin, 21 percent of iron, 18 percent of bauxite, and 14 percent of nickel. Its oil reserves are also important: one-third of world's production of bioethanol, around 25 percent of biofuels, and 13 percent of oil comes from this region.

Almost 30 percent of the total renewable water resources in the world are in the region, representing more than 70 percent of the water on the South American continent, as well as 21 percent of the planet's forests and abundant biodiversity. However, the region also has flaws, such as there are fewer investments and focus on renewable resources or sustainable investments. Because the main objective is quicker results without consideration for the future or environmental impact, Latin America remains far from developing sustainable production. Latin America also has a general delay in innovation in science and technology.[25]

The arrival to power of several nationalist governments in Latin America is changing the rules of the game in the energy market, compelling foreign companies to share the profits earned from high prices of hydrocarbons (oil and gas) more equitably. This was the case in Bolivia with the arrival of President Evo Morales, who ordered military occupation of 56 oil and gas fields in the country and nationalization of other natural resources.

In Venezuela, President Hugo Chavez forced companies to sign operational agreements to create joint enterprises with a majority state ownership, increased royalties on hydrocarbons through a law reform passed in 2001, and demanded a payment of 50 percent of income taxes instead of 34 percent. Ecuador passed a law that added an additional 50 percent tax on foreign oil companies' revenues from the extraction of oil, the main export product of that country. In Argentina, oil companies experienced a boycott for having increased their prices.

Contrary to this trend in Latin America, is Mexico, another major oil producer in the region, with a volume of nearly three million barrels per day. Mexico exports around 60 percent of its oil, mostly to the United States. Mexican oil production is controlled by state-owned Pemex, which is beginning to allow the participation of foreign capital, a process that in the long-run would end in privatization.

Although Latin America faces an enormous number of issues with women, children, indigenous people, health, housing, and education, it is important to look at the region and its people in light of its actions and struggles to overcome historical challenges, inequalities, and injustice.

There are many initiatives from the governments and also from civil society as nongovernmental organizations (NGOs), churches, and others are making an attempt to address the issues and have achieved some success. One great achievement is the number of people who are living above the poverty line, getting more education and in many countries, such as Brazil, are gaining access to more employment opportunities, as a result of the Bolsa Família and other programs.

There have been some improvements made in certain areas, such as prevention of violence against youth by NGO efforts, including Sou da Paz in Brazil and Caminando por La Paz (Walking for Peace) in Guatemala. Also, there are a great number of organizations and people who work with education, arts, and culture, in places that lack adequate education and access to cultural events. The numbers of people, organizations, and churches that work individually or as institutions are growing, each one of them doing its part to help Latin America overcome its challenges. Although the problems are complex, there are people who are strong, determined, vigorous, and work hard to address the historical inequities. Latin America is a place with a people as rich, strong, and hopeful as its land.

This New World, the land that the colonists called Latin America, and its people have the strength and the willingness to overcome historical issues and to build a new future that could offer better living to all.

The next two chapters will explore the role of culture, religion, and faith, and how Latin Americans are working to help overcome the historical challenges.

A student studies in a classroom in Batey Bombita. The community, located in southwest Dominican Republic, is populated by Haitian immigrants and their descendants. *(Paul Jeffrey)*

A woman looking in a mirror gets her hair styled outdoors in Mizak, a small village in the south of Haiti.

(Paul Jeffrey)

Profiles

Cândido

"Have you ever tried cocoa honey? This is what you do: you open the cocoa bean, put it this way…sideways… and leave it. The honey will flow—that's cocoa honey. You have to eat it soon… it's sweet… very sweet. If you leave it longer, it will be good only to make other sweets later. I was born with cocoa."

Cândido comes from a large family of nine siblings. He was born in northeastern Brazil, in the Caatinga scrub forest of Bahia, a dry land that suffers from the lack of water. The first city where he and his family lived was Santa Cruz da Vitória, which is in a cattle-breeding area. "My mother used to wake me up at dawn to go and steal water from a dam nearby." When he was eight, the family moved to the south of Bahia, where they lived on a cocoa production farm. After a few years, they went to Ibirapitanga, a city near Salvador, where he stayed until he was 15.

In the 1980s, he came to São Paulo to live with one of his sisters in Jardim Ângela, a neighborhood in the south of São Paulo, which had the highest homicide rate in the city; it was even considered one of the most violent places in the world in 1995, according to a study by Sérgio Adorno, a professor at Universidade de São Paulo. That was during the "peak of unemployment," the end of a dictatorship, and a time of recession.

Cândido didn't have a steady job for a whole year. He did odd jobs and work as a hod carrier. In 1981, he got a job as a metalworker's assistant making large iron structures and tanks. In 1996, when metallurgy went downhill, "I changed to the educational field," he says. He started working in a daycare center where he was responsible for maintenance. In 2005, Cândido went to work for a nongovernmental institution that is also in the educational field. When he talks about his work he says, "In the daycare, I was useful for a thousand things.

Now I am for 1001." He takes care of plants, cleaning, electrical and hydraulic maintenance, and also proudly collaborates on other projects. He was even invited to contribute to the institution's projects by writing a text. He says, "I'm collaborating with education. Someone might read what I've written."

Why São Paulo? "There are some who say it's an illusion about the market, the best way to earn a living. If you are in the north or in the northeast of the country, you have no perspective on life, not even the things you plant produce anything, grow. Drought kills even the workers. . . . Everybody wants to have a better life. Here we have jobs and it's enough to survive. São Paulo offers better opportunities for people to live; at least we can get jobs."

And how was his arrival to the city? According to Cândido, "In the past, people were stranded due to lack of communication, but now the media gives a lot of information.

"When we first arrived, people would swarm like bees to help each other to build houses. When you see at the top a raised roof, you think, 'I helped to build that one.' That exchange of experiences is priceless."

He's been married for 22 years and loves going out to dance Forró, a genre of Brazilian music that originated in northeastern Brazil. His wife, Dedina, also came from Bahia and she is a distant cousin. Says Candido, "One day she went to visit her aunt's house and I was there." At that time, Dedina already had a three-year-old son, and Cândido helped to raise the child, who calls him Dad. Together, he and Dedina had two more children.

Cândido likes to wake up early. He takes the bus and the subway to go to work, a journey that can take one hour and forty minutes, which can be delayed up to three and a half hours in a lot of traffic. He doesn't like to be idle. He gives talks at Catholic churches (as a member of the Couples for Christ group), where he discusses how to "dialogue with children" (above all, teenagers—how to approach them, when you should get closer and when you need to give them limits) and "responsible parenthood" by telling about his experience of having welcomed his wife's first son. He also participates in social movements seeking to improve his neighborhood, and especially on how to decrease violence.

Anne

"I'm not the kind of person who would leave São Paulo, but I fell in love with the project I work in." Anne is 26 years old and a journalism graduate. She worked as a web designer for social networks and new media. She has also participated in state and community projects. Two years ago, she took part in a study group on journalism and technology. She was invited to be part of the team for a new project in the Pantanal and at Serra da Bodoquena, in the central-west region of Brazil, with the idea of creating new networks of communicators through journalism workshops, which included the study of human rights and video coverage, among other themes. Nowadays she lives in Bonito, a city that promotes eco-tourism in the central-west region of Brazil.

Anne's mother became pregnant when she was 17 years old, and ran away from Bahia, a state in the northeast of Brazil, to São Paulo, where she started to work as a housemaid and lived at her employers' house. The families were getting annoyed about housing a child at home, and Anne went to Bahia to live with her aunt. After one year, her mother changed her job in order to be near her daughter.

For her mother, studying education was a priority. She saved money and faced hard times so that her daughter could go to college. Anne took the entrance exam in 2004 and was approved and, with the encouragement from her mother, she got a scholarship from Prouni, a program by the Brazilian Federal Government that finances college education for low-income youth. She

is the first person in the family to be admitted to attend a university. She says, "My mother gave me the foundation for this to happen."

Anne emphasizes the beauty of the city of Bonito, located in the state of Mato Grosso, in the central-west region of Brazil, where she lives now. "Here, there is nothing that can stop you from seeing the sky. The sky is always light blue, and everything matches that blue, especially the toucans, which are abundant."

Five-year-old Eline Medjune, a girl in an orphanage in Leogane, Haiti, gives a kiss to Elena Bargo, a Spanish woman who lives in New York. Bargo is helping care for the children here as a volunteer with the Dominican-Haitian Women's Movement (MUDHA). *(Paul Jeffrey)*

Endnotes

1. David Ferranti et al., "Inequality in Latin America and the Caribbean: Breaking with History? Advance Conference Copy" (Washington, DC: World Bank, October 2003), www.cepal.org/ilpes/noticias/paginas/7/29107/inequality_latin_america_complete.pdf.

2. "Inequality in Latin America and the Caribbean," *Global Policy Forum*, last modified October 8, 2003, www.globalpolicy.org/component/content/article/218-injustice-and-inequality/46540.html.

3. "The Social Panorama of Latin America 2012," Social Development Division and the Statistics Division of the Economic Commission for Latin America and the Caribbean (ECLAC), www.eclac.org/cgi-bin/getProd.asp?xml=/publicaciones/xml/4/48454/P48454.xml&xsl=/publicaciones/ficha-i.xsl&base=/publicaciones/top_publicaciones-i.xsl.

4. David Ferranti et al., "Inequality in Latin America and the Caribbean: Breaking with History? Advance Conference Copy."

5. Ibid.

6. "The State of Latin American and Caribbean Cities 2012," *UN-Habitat*, August 2012, www.unhabitat.org/pmss/listItemDetails.aspx?publicationID=3386.

7. Ibid.

8. Ibid.

9. Ibid.

10. "Violence Against Women Factsheet," *United Nations Population Fund (UNFPA)*, accessed October 20, 2014, www.unfpa.org/swp/2005/presskit/factsheets/facts_vaw.htm.

11. "Breaking the Silence on Violence against Indigenous Girls, Adolescents and Young Women," United Nations Children's Fund (UNICEF), the United Nations Entity for Gender Equality and the Empowerment of Women (UN Women), the United Nations Population Fund (UNFPA), the International Labour Organization (ILO) and the Office of the Special Representative of the Secretary-General on Violence against Children (OSRSG/VAC), May 2013, www.unwomen.org/~/media/headquarters/attachments/sections/library/publications/2013/5/violence-against-indigenous-women-and-girls.pdf.

12. Ibid.

13. Ibid.

14. Ibid.

15. "Indigenous Peoples in Latin America—A General Overview," *International Work Group for Indigenous Affairs*, accessed August 13, 2013, www.iwgia.org/regions/latin-america/indigenous-peoples-in-latin-america.

16. Ibid.

17. Luis Ferreira, "A diáspora africana na América Latina e o Caribe," accessed August 13, 2013, afrolatinos.palmares.gov.br/_temp/sites/000/6/download/artigos/artigo-Luis%20Ferreira.pdf.

18. Edward Telles and Lisa Steele, "Pigmentocracy in the Americas: How is Educational Attainment Related to Skin Color?" accessed August 20, 2013, www.vanderbilt.edu/lapop/insights/IO873en.pdf.

19. Darién J. Davis, United Nations Higher Commissioner, "Latin America: Afro-descendants," accessed August 22, 2013, www.refworld.org/pdfid/4795b32e1f.pdf.

20. Ibid.

21. Julio Jacobo Waiselfisz, *Mapa da Violência 2013—Homicídios e Juventude no Brasil* (Rio de Janeiro: Flacso and Cebela, 2013), 72.

22. Sérgio Adorno, "Crianças e adolescentes e a violência urbana," *Sociologias* [online], n.8 (2002), www.scielo.br/scielo.php?script=sci_arttext&pid=S1517-45222002000200005, 122.

23. Waiselfisz, *Mapa da Violência 2013—Homicídios e Juventude no Brasil*, 5.

24. Eduardo Galeano, *Open Veins of Latin America: Five Centuries of the Pillage of a Continent*, 25th anniversary ed. (New York: Monthly Review Press, 1997), 12.

25. R. M. Auty, *Sustaining Development in Mineral Economies: The Resource Curse Thesis* (London: Routledge, 1993) 181.

A young Haitian-Dominican woman performs liturgical dance during worship in an evangelical church in La Hoya, a small rural town near Barahona in the southwest of the Dominican Republic. The service brought together Dominicans and Haitian-Dominicans from a nearby batey in an unusual demonstration of unity in a land where discrimination against Dominicans of Haitian ancestry is growing. *(Paul Jeffrey)*

Chapter 4

Culture, Art, and Women in Politics

This chapter will give an overview of Latin America's diverse culture, art, music, dance, and visual arts. It will present the primary customs and lifestyles of families living in Latin America. The chapter also will demonstrate how women in Latin America have been a strong social and political force, and how they have been working to overcome the many challenges they face in the region.

A Culture as Diverse as the Land

Culture reveals the differences in living, as well as lifestyles, values, and customs of a society, and it also ensures the connection between people and institutions, spaces and times. It links a person to a community, to a group, and to a place, and also to their history, so that people get to know how to behave and what to expect in certain spaces. People express their culture in many ways; for example, by the clothes they wear, their music, and way of speaking, or how they eat. Through his or her culture, a person can feel integrated or not with the community's way of thinking and how the community behaves. It is the commonality of experience, beliefs, and history that connects a community, alive and in continuous movement. Culture provides people with a web of connection to each other, and helps to interpret, update, modify, and include new concepts that can define and influence the community in the future.

As a vast land, Latin America holds valuable wealth, not only from a material standpoint, but also of historical and social significance. There are myriad manifestations of culture that have ancestral origins. Latin America is a fusion of cultures, ethnic groups, and peoples due to the mixing of the cultures—indigenous, African, and European—all of whom were already living there or arrived in the region.

As a result of its history, Latin America is comprised of diverse cultures and ethnic groups with specific characteristics. In order to have a clear panorama of their cultural manifestations, it is important to consider the differences of each group and highlight the main aspects of their cultural diversity and integration. We will examine the social, economic, political, cultural, and historical characteristics of each country. Here you will find highlights of various cultural expressions in the different countries.

Roots of Art and Culture in Latin America

It can be said that pre-Columbian civilizations established roots of art and culture in Latin America. Each one of these indigenous civilizations, as was seen in Chapter 1, developed their own culture and artistic expressions, highly influenced by the social context, religious and spiritual concerns, and beliefs.

During the time of colonization, most historical and cultural landmarks of these civilizations were destroyed. Today there are only remains of the pre-Columbian period. It is possible to find a few buildings and objects of religious use, such as sculptures and paintings, and household ornamental objects, amulets, and fabrics. The study of these objects and constructions, findings as well as their identification, the systems used and what they represented to the people helps us to better understand the pre-Columbian cultures.

The peak of Mayan culture occurred between the years 300 and 900 AD, with the presence of highly skilled architects and engineers, sculptors and painters, who developed advanced numerical and astronomical systems, and created hieroglyphic writing and a complex calendar.

Mayan sculptures and paintings featured representations of stylized human figures, with geometric features and animal forms. In the paintings, the use of symbols or figures was common. Mayan artists used colors to symbolize some situations or states of mind; for example, black was the color of war, and yellow indicated fertility. In the Mayan pantheon, Itzamna is the chief god, considered the creator of the calendar, writing, and the number system. Stone was the primary material the Mayan used for their architecture, and both stone and clay were used for sculpture.

The Mayan people are also are known for the organization of their cities and buildings that were arranged around courtyards and differed according to the administrative function. Many of the Mayan constructions in general were used for religious or ceremonial purposes, and many of the surviving structures are grandiose. Generally, Mayan buildings that housed the common population were low in height, in contrast to the pyramid forms upon which were built temples and palaces that rose to impressive heights. The massive stones of the buildings and the steps that lead up to the top of the temples were carefully cut so that they fit perfectly together. The buildings were designed to be symmetrical, with the steep steps often bisecting the center of the facade.

The Mayans developed an innovative form of architecture by creating "false roofs" (corbeled arches), used to cover hallways, rooms, and graves. Great attention was paid to the exteriors of the monuments, temples, and palaces, which were richly ornamented with figures and hieroglyphic characters carved in relief.

At some Mayan architectural sites, astronomical observatories have been discovered, such as El Caracol in the city of Chichén Itzá (Mexico). The sites also reveal the existence of ball courts, plazas, and a well-planned urban infrastructure. The Governor's Palace in Uxmal (Mexico), temples, and monumental buildings and sculptures from the cities of Copán (Honduras) and Tikal (Guatemala) are among the sites of major Mayan ruins.

The Aztecs or *Mexica* inherited some elements of Mayan art and culture, such as the temples in the shape of pyramids constructed on platforms. Their capital city, Tenochtitlán, was built on an artificial island located in Lake Texcoco, with Templo Mayor one of its primary buildings. As the Aztec people were predominantly warriors, militarism influenced many aspects of their constructions as well as their religious life. Accordingly, martial conquests were dedicated to their main gods. Aztec rites and iconography of liturgical art involved the sacrifice of prisoners and was also related to war. Therefore, much of the art of the Aztecs has a macabre air. It is common to find human skull masks ornamented with clay or semiprecious stones, as well as the representation of heads and skulls with empty eye sockets.

Many of the sculptures were carved from massive stones and decorated with stylized designs. Aztecs artists and craftsmen were known for their great manual skill. There are still in existence many objects of their work in metal and precious stone, as well as rich feather art and garment fabrics with geometric motifs in rich colors, as well as murals and miniatures painted on strips of deerskin.

The Incas lived around Lake Titicaca, in the region of the central Andes of Peru. They began their expansion and supremacy in 1438 from their capital, Cusco, in southern Peru. The Incas were primarily an agricultural people. They invented the *quipu*, based on a tool made of wool strings of various colors and sizes used as an accounting system, but did not develop a written language. The Incas created ceramics both ceremonial and utilitarian, some decorated with geometric designs and others finely ornamented incorporating animal motifs.

Cloth played an important role in Inca culture and was used for trading. Woven from wool sheared from llamas and alpacas or the finest wool from vicuñas, dyes made from plants provided a variety of bright colors, or the cloth was the natural brown, gray, and white of the wool from which it was woven. The Incas were among the skilled metallurgists of the Andean region, creating finely decorated objects of gold, silver, and bronze for adornment and ceremonial functions. Later, bronze was used in weapons and tools.[1]

The architectural features of Inca buildings emphasize simplicity and organization and, as in the fortress Sacsayhuaman that guarded Cusco, massive stones were used in their construction. Cusco was a complex urban center planned with distinct religious and administrative functions, surrounded by clearly delineated areas for agricultural and industrial production. One of the most familiar icons of Inca culture, Machu Picchu was a site built around 1450, as is believed to have been an estate for the Inca emperor Pachacuti. Located nearly 8,000 feet above sea level atop a mountain, it is also theorized that Machu Picchu was a sacred religious site because of its location. It's been noted that the rising and setting of the sun, which the Incas considered a god, when viewed from certain locations within the site aligns with religiously significant mountains during solstices and equinoxes. The Incas lacked strong draft animals and did not employ the wheel in their engineering. How they moved and placed the enormous blocks of stone in the construction of Machu Picchu remains unknown.

Art in the Colonial Period

The initial arrival of the Spanish and the Portuguese, and then other European immigrants, brought to the new continent their language, culture, and religious customs, which were imposed on the indigenous inhabitants of the continent. Thus, artistic creativity during the colonial period was significantly influenced by the colonizers' style and trends. This was a period, in many ways a process, of suppression and destruction of native artistic expressions, such as their pre-Columbian architecture, cultural, and religious manifestations.

In this sense, the art that developed in the colonies was very similar to what was happening in Europe, or at least in the stream of artistic styles that prevailed in this period, such as baroque, rococo, and neoclassicism.

For the art historian Dawn Ades, who wrote *Art in Latin America* (*Arte na America Latina*), the arrival of the conquerors brought about a change in the architecture, with the construction of buildings, such as cathedrals, villas, hospitals, private homes, most often in the European style.[2]

To mark the settlers' supremacy in religion, some of the Roman Catholic churches were built on top of ancient indigenous temples. The construction of the Cathedral of Cusco, located in the Plaza de Armas, was started in 1560 and lasted over a hundred years. The main structure of the church was raised on the palace of the Inca god Wiracocha. Besides using many blocks of stones from the fortress of Sacsayhuaman for elevation, they used indigenous people for the manual labor, thus the Roman Catholic Church left its mark forever. In the cathedral is a painting by Marcos Zapata, a Peruvian Quechua painter born in Cusco, who was taught by Spanish painters. The painting, *The Last Supper*, shows Christ and the disciples gathered around the table at the center of which the dish about to be served is a roasted cuy, similar to the guinea pig and a delicacy in Cusco during Inca times. In the choir, there are seats with slots that refer to Pachamama, Mother Earth in the Andean tradition.

Ades studied the building of the historical churches in Latin America and explains that in 1571 the Jesuits decided to build the Church of the Society of Jesus (Iglesia de La Compañía de Jesús) also in Cusco, Peru, at Amarucancha, the former palace of the Inca emperor Huayna Capac. Located in the Plaza de Armas next to the Cathedral, the church is one of the most beautiful samples of Andean Baroque. With the earthquake of 1650, the religious temple underwent a rebuilding process that lasted until 1688. Even during colonization, this church was emblematic of a place of the first marriages performed in Cusco, such as the union of Beatriz Clara Coya, Inca princess, daughter of Sayri Huarcay Cusi and Tupac, and Martín García de Loyola, nephew of San Ignacio de Loyola who founded the Compañía de Jesús. A painting commissioned at the time of the wedding can be seen in the church today.

The Metropolitan Cathedral of the Assumption of Mary in Mexico City, one of the oldest and largest Roman Catholic cathedrals in Latin America, is another example of building on former sacred Indigenous places. It is situated atop the former Aztec sacred place, the Templo Mayor (Large Temple).[3]

For the English historian Leslie Bethell, founder of the Centre for Brazilian Studies at the University of Oxford, the architecture and the fine arts of South America have been strongly influenced by European designs, mainly Portuguese and Spanish; while on the other hand, cuisine, music, and many of the customs have been influenced by native cultures. According to him, in general, Mexico, Central America, and the Antilles form the more open areas directly influenced by the Spanish.[4]

Some regions of South America, such as the city of Quito, Ecuador, have attracted large numbers of religions that came to the New World from other European countries, as well as many architects and painters. In other places in South America, such as in Peru in the mountains around Arequipa, Callao, and the cities of the plain, even up to Cusco and Potosi, the pre-Columbian art and culture were better preserved.[5]

Art during the Nineteenth and Twentieth Centuries

The artistic expression in Latin America was greatly influenced by European trends, primarily Classicism, Romanticism, and Realism, taught in various academies founded during the colonial period that continued through the era of independence. Some well-known artists of the independence period are the Argentines Eduardo Sívori, Prilidiano Pueyrredón, and Ernesto de la Cárcova; the Chileans Pedro Lira and Alfredo

Valenzuela Puelma; the Brazilians Victor Meirelles and Manuel de Araújo Porto-Alegre; and the Mexicans Santiago Rebull and José María Velasco Gómez, among others.

According to Ades, in the beginning of the twentieth century, art in Latin America began to inspire other artistic movements that were emerging within European Modernism, including Cubism, Constructivism, Surrealism, and Dadaism, which assumed different expressions according to the individual artist. Most of the artists had the opportunity to study in Europe, but as they returned to their homeland they adopted the techniques and artistic trends of the surrounding region and began to create art with more Latin American expressions and local influences.[6]

It was a time of great vitality; one example was the Mexican Revolution, which was immortalized in murals by painters who helped to disseminate the revolutionary and nationalist ideas, like Diego Rivera. In general, these artists helped spread a sense of cultural nationalism in Latin American countries and have had a lasting influence on the culture of the region. Some groups created magazines such as *Klaxon* (1922) and the *Revista de Antropafagia* (1928) in Brazil, *Actual* and *Machete* in Mexico, *Martín Fierro* in Argentina, and *Amauta* in Peru.

Among the artists who stand out in this period in Latin America are the already mentioned, Diego Rivera, as well as David Alfaro Siqueiros, José Clemente Orozco, Rufino Tamayo, and Frida Kahlo from Mexico; Pedro Nel Gómez and Santiago Martínez Delgado from Colombia; the Uruguayan Joaquín Torres García; the Cuban Wifredo Lam; Roberto Matta from Chile; and the Brazilians Tarsila do Amaral, Anita Malfatti, and Cândido Portinari.[7]

Today, Latin American painting is highly heterogeneous and individual. Among the artists in the region who excel internationally are the Argentinian León Ferrari, Brazilians Vik Muniz and Cildo Meireles, Chilean

Maria Brigida Gonzalez, a member of the Peace Community of San José de Apartadó, Colombia. In 1997, 1,400 war-weary peasants declared they would no longer cooperate with any of the armed parties in the hemisphere's longest-running war. They paid a heavy price for their witness; more than 200 members of the community have been killed. In 2013, two army generals were indicted for a 2005 massacre in the community. On December 10, 2013, President Juan Manuel Santos, in the name of the state, publicly asked the community for forgiveness.

(Paul Jeffrey)

Claudio Bravo, Colombian Fernando Botero, Ecuadoran Oswaldo Guayasamín, Mexicans Francisco Toledo, Manuel Felguérez, José Luis Cuevas, Pedro Friedeberg, Ignacio Barrios, Jorge Marín, and Luis Nishizawa, Peruvians Teodoro Núñez Ureta and Fernando de Szyszlo, among many others.[8]

Ancient Traditions, Values, and Knowledge

In the field of visual arts, the appreciation of local cultures began with the Modernists in the early twentieth century. This was a great improvement, considering that culture in Latin America produced by the encounter of African and indigenous cultures had always been disregarded. According to anthropologist José Jorge Carvalho, even the term "indigenous" had been associated with the idea of savage or barbaric, as if they did not have culture, or that their values and knowledge were irrelevant as they were not considered civilized. A similar reasoning was applied to people originating in Africa who came as slaves to Latin America. Their knowledge, cultures, art, and technology were also disregarded as even their human condition was not recognized.[9]

According to Carvalho, this disregard generated among these people as a feeling of devaluation and alienation, which resulted in their search for spaces of resistance to face their life of hardship and suffering and to preserve their cultural identity and inherent knowledge. Indigenous peoples preserved and passed on their knowledge of the fauna and flora and its medicinal and religious uses through their oral traditions.[10]

Enslaved Africans came from different regions of Africa, with distinct languages, customs, and religions. They had to almost entirely redo and recreate their knowledge and cultural codes, and they also had to adapt those to living in the colonies or when they escaped and formed marooned societies. In other cases, they managed to incorporate the cultural symbols and codes of the European settlers and adapted them. This can be seen, for example, in religion when Catholic saints are identified with entities of African religion that we will study in

Chapter 5. Thus, when talking about Latin American culture, one must keep in mind that this is not a homogeneous culture, but diverse, complex, and replete with a mixing of different cultures and influences, which some refer to as the mestizo culture, or hybrid.

More recently, African and indigenous groups have begun to recognize their inherent knowledge and traditional values as a means to realize their identity, culture, and social values.

Among the traditional artifacts of the region the following can be highlighted:

Pottery
The oldest artistic and utilitarian expression of human culture, pottery was crafted throughout pre-Columbian civilizations. In Mexico, there is now an export market for pottery. Mexican ceramics have fine details, some incorporating colorful glazes and design techniques that were adapted during the colonial period. Other pottery is produced with surfaces that are burnished rather than glazed and painted with fine clay slips, traditional techniques that have been passed down from parents to children, originating with their historic Aztec and Mayan ancestors. In northern Peru, the pottery produced in and near the town of Chulucanas is exported worldwide. Predating the Incan empire, the pottery designs are predominantly black and white, and have been passed down through the generations.[11]

Fabrics
The colorful textiles found mainly in Spanish Latin America have their origin in the sacred traditions passed down through generations by the indigenous people groups. They started using cotton to produce the textiles but as the technology and practice advanced, the Andean people primarily began using wool shorn from alpacas, vicuñas, and llamas, animals typically found in the high mountains. It is important to point out the important role of women and children in this process. They are often in charge of caring for the animals, herding the

flock, gathering the wool, and also dyeing and weaving the colorful fabrics.

The dyeing of the fabrics employed ancient techniques to create the colors based on knowledge passed from one generation to the next. For instance, to make blue, a combination of the root of the tara plant and blue copa, or the leaves of the indigo plant were used; red was made from cochinillina (an insect typically found on cactus in the region); to make the color green, ch'illca (a green plant) was used in combination with other plants; and to make yellow, qolle flowers from the region were used.[12]

Basketry

The weaving of baskets from vegetable fibers is one of the most ancient and widespread art forms in Latin America. While ceramics were created as vessels for food and drink, woven basketry generally served as a pliable and lightweight means of transporting fruits, vegetables, as well as dry goods.[13]

In Mexico, many indigenous populations developed this art, as did the Tarahumara, or Rarámuri, of Copper Canyon. They typically weave with pine needles and sotol fiber, a plant that grows in northern Mexico. In the Amazon region the Yanomami paint their woven tray and burden baskets with geometric designs using charcoal and a red berry dye. In general, women are the main basket weavers. They create baskets in a wide range of styles, shapes, and sizes, some as much as two feet wide, and feature tight weaves with an impressive array of designs.[14]

Dance

Latin American folk music and dance is a mix of the people's diversity with influences of colonial European, indigenous, and African cultures. These influences have different ratios according to each country or region and present a wide variety of original expression. For example, the music of Central America and the Andean highlands is strongly evocative of indigenous rhythms and dances that existed before the arrival of the conquerors. The influence of African rhythms is especially heard in tropical and coastal areas: West Indies, Cuba, Venezuela, Colombia, and Brazil, where most African slaves had arrived. Read on for some musical rhythms and dance developed in Latin America.[15]

Venezuela and Colombia

The joropo is a dance like the waltz, with African influences, which is very common in both Venezuela and Colombia. The joropo tap is characterized by the strong paces of the man and the softer steps of the woman. The dancers stand in a circle and spin backwards clockwise forming traditional figures. In general, the instruments that accompany joropo are mandolin, a kind of viola, harp, and maracas. This dance is part of the celebrations of the *Cruz de Mayo* celebration in the eastern region of Venezuela.

Caribbean

The origins of calypso go back to the nineteenth century and the islands of Trinidad and Tobago. It is considered Afro-Caribbean music. Calypso has a beat that had been widely used as a means of communication among slaves. Because they could not talk to each other, they would talk through the music. The beat ended up influencing other rhythms like salsa. Calypso spread widely in the region and is present in virtually all countries of Central America and the Caribbean; some believe that it was the influence of calypso that led to reggae.

Another rhythm with origins in the Caribbean is zouk, which had begun in the French Antilles (Martinique, Guadeloupe, and Saint Lucia) and has spread and is now present in countries of Central America and Brazil.

The rumba is a musical genre that started in Cuba and is also strongly influenced by African rhythms that have impacted other genres like mambo, cha-mambo, cha-cha, and salsa, which are very popular in Puerto Rico and throughout the Spanish-speaking countries.

The merengue is a popular dance of the Dominican Republic and Dominica, but also performed in Puerto Rico, Haiti, Venezuela, and Colombia. It is considered fast paced and mischievous with spicy lyrics and dancing with partners always held very close. It got its name from Merengue, the name given by the Dominicans to the French invaders.[16]

Brazil

The samba is a musical rhythm born out of the mix of musical styles from Africa and Brazil. It is played primarily with percussion instruments including drums, and accompanied by guitar and ukulele. Generally, the lyrics express everyday situations, especially of the urban poor. The samba is widespread in Brazil, with many regional variations and influences expanding its theme, and has become one of Brazil's national symbols. It has a main rhythm, which is based in the Brazilian Carnival, a large festivity celebrated throughout the country.[17]

Art and Resistance under Dictatorships

There was a gloomy period in the region's history during the military dictatorships in Latin America. During this time of oppression, resistance was not tolerated and those who did were ruthlessly crushed. The military dictatorships were very harsh, especially with those who dared to challenge their governing style. For many, art was a way to express resistance. Artists all over Latin America raised their voices for freedom through music, theater, and the visual arts.

Some examples of the artists who took a stand against the dictatorship regimes and the oppression mainly of the poor people in Latin America were writers such as Uruguayan Eduardo Galeano, who wrote *The Open Veins of Latin America*, where he denounces the exploitation of the Latin American territory. Singers including the Argentine Mercedes Sosa, Brazilian Geraldo Vandré, the Chileans Violeta Parra and Victor Jara. After the military coup in Chile, Victor was arrested, tortured, shot, and his body abandoned in a slum in Santiago, Chile. They were some of the voices who fought military oppression at the time.[18] Many of the artists, politicians, teachers, and students were arrested, tortured, killed, or exiled. There was and still is a huge contingent of those who speak out against oppression in Latin America.

One example of music that was an expression of resistance at that time was the song "Canción con Todos" by Armando Tejada Gómez, sung by Mercedes Sosa, which was a hallmark of union and resistance during that period. Below is an excerpt of the song:

Canción con Todos
by Armando Tejada Gómez

Sol de alto Perú
Rostro Bolivia, estaño y soledad
Un verde Brasil besa a mi Chile
Cobre y mineral
Subo desde el sur
Hacia la entraña América y total
Pura raíz de un grito
Destinado a crecer
Y a estallar.
Todas las voces, todas
Todas las manos, todas
Toda la sangre puede
Ser canción en el viento.
¡Canta conmigo, canta
Hermano americano
Libera tu esperanza
Con un grito en la voz!

Song with Everything
(Translation by Amanda M. Bachus)

Sun of High Peru
Face of Bolivia, tin and solitude
A green Brazil kisses my Chile
Copper and mineral
I ascend from the south
Towards the Américas womb, whole
The purest root of a scream
Destined to grow
And to break out
All voices, all
All hands, all
All the blood can
Be a song in the wind.

Sing with me, sing!
American brother
Liberate your hope
With a loud cry in your voice!

"Canción con Todos," by Armando Tejada Gómez.
Used with permission.

The Role of Women in Culture, Art, and Politics

Latin American women's history and their participation in art and culture are fragmented, and there are several issues to cover and to identify regarding their contributions to the arts, culture, and the economy of the region. According to the Roger Thayer Stone Center for Latin American Studies at Tulane University, which has been collecting a wide range of materials, books, videos, and articles about women in Latin America, the researchers in Latin America:

> …must address the cultural achievements of women. As far back as the seventeenth century, women have distinguished themselves as outstanding poets, novelists, painters, and musicians. Juana Inés de la Cruz (Sor Juana) was a well-known poet in Mexico in the mid-1600s. In many cases, female artists have gained both national and international recognition for their work. For instance, the Chilean novelist Gabriela Mistral was awarded the Nobel Prize for literature in 1945, the first Latin American writer and a woman. Other writers include Isabel Allende, Julia Alvarez, Sandra Cisneros, Laura Esquivel, Silvina Ocampo, Cristina Peri Rossi, Daisy Zamora, Gioconda Belli, Vida Luz, Clarice Lispector, Raquel de Queiroz, Cecília Meireles, and Elena Poniatowska as well as many others.[19]

Gender and Family Roles

Although gender role and societal expectations of men and women are important issues in all cultures, in Latin America they have been shaped largely by cultural-specific values and beliefs, the family life, and how it is organized in Latin America.

The Stone Center for Latin American Studies at Tulane University has been studying this issue and points out that the terms "machismo" and "marianismo" (originating from the cult of Mary, mother of Jesus) "...describe the set of ideal attributes of males and females (respectively) that has developed in the region. Machismo is defined as the cult of male virility, in which the ideal man is bold, intransigent, and sexually aggressive," while the women have to be holy following the steps of Mary as a model, they are supposed to be more passive, demure, and accepting of life's suffering.[20]

Researchers affirm, on the other hand, that marianismo refers to the cult of feminine moral superiority, which defines the ideal woman as selfless, submissive, and possessing great spiritual strength. The Virgin Mary is widely viewed as the epitome of femininity, and is held up as a model to which Latin American women should aspire. Machismo and marianismo not only outline the expectations of men and women in Latin America, they also serve to establish and reinforce the sexual division of labor. Because women are expected to be nurturing and morally superior to men, they have been assigned to duties associated with the family, in particular the rearing and education of children. In short, they have been relegated to the private sphere.

But despite this mind-set, which assigns a subordinate place to women "female power and influence can be quite extensive. Men, by virtue of their supposed strength and assertiveness, are given exclusive domain over the public sphere (i.e., politics, the economy, international affairs, etc.). As a result, they are dismissed from any responsibility in the home."[21]

Family is probably the main space in which values and behaviors are shaped, reproduced, and are passed through generations, especially the mind-set about the roles of men and women. According to the researchers from Tulane University, family has traditionally been an important institution in Latin America. Women play a central role in the organization and maintenance of family life and traditions. In discussing the Latin American family, it is essential to emphasize that families come in a wide range of forms and sizes, different from the main model in North America where "nuclear family" is more common.[22]

In literature we find some examples of the complexity in family settings as in Gabriel García Márquez's *One Hundred Years of Solitude* and Isabel Allende's *The House of Spirits*, which are two well-known novels that recount the histories of traditional, extended families. These novels are excellent examples of "magical realism," a style in twentieth-century literature that developed in Latin America.

Women and Politics

Political activism has been a common role for women in Latin America. Women participated in suffrage battles since the nineteenth century when they fought to obtain the right to vote. In most Latin American countries, women won the right to vote in the 1940s and 50s. Ever since, many women have run for political office in countries throughout Latin America. Isabel Martínez de Perón was the first female president of a country in Latin America when she was elevated from vice president to president of Argentina after the death of her husband, Juan Perón. She governed Argentina and held office from 1974 to 1976 when the democratically elected government was overthrown by a military coup. Argentina continues to have active women politicians. Cristina Fernández de Kirchner was elected to the presidency in 2007.

Many other Latin American countries have had female heads of state including Bolivia when Lidia Gueiler Tejada, head of the Chamber of Deputies, became interim president after elections held in 1979 did not reach majority of votes. Congress elected her due to her position as head of the Chamber. Gueiler Tejada held the presidential post for a period of eight months (1979–1980) when a military coup removed her from power and she left the country.

In Chile, Michelle Bachelet served as president from 2006 to 2010, and was reelected for a second term in 2013. In Brazil, Dilma Rousseff was elected president in 2011 and again in 2014; and in Costa Rica, Laura Chinchilla was elected president in 2010.

In Nicaragua, Violeta Chamorro served as president from 1990 to 1997, defeating Daniel Ortega and bringing in a time of peace after an eleven-year civil war.

Political activism in Latin America has not been confined to the political office. Women have engaged in protests, work strikes, hunger strikes, and in some countries armed insurgencies. In recent decades, women have taken a leading role in grassroots political movements aimed at achieving social and economic justice in the region.

Many Latin American women see absolutely no contradiction between their political commitments and their duties as wives and mothers. In general, women commonly view their political activism as an extension of their traditional gender roles. In those cases where the political and/or economic situation of their country threatens the well-being of their families, women often see themselves as having an obligation to become politically involved.

This kind of political involvement of women in South America gained momentum during the military regimes of the 1970s and 1980s. Argentina, Brazil, Chile, and Uruguay were ruled by military regimes, which employed violent tactics against their citizens to achieve social order and economic progress. Individuals suspected of engaging in subversive activities were kidnapped (or "disappeared"), tortured, or assassinated by the military and right wing paramilitary groups. Women mobilized in large numbers in efforts to demand that the government provide them with information about their missing husbands and children.

Numerous documentaries recount these women's struggles for social justice. Madres de Plaza de Mayo

(Mothers of the Plaza de Mayo) is an organization of Argentinian women that marched each week in the capital's main plaza to protest the disappearance of their spouses and children, many of whom disappeared during the period of dictatorship. This group gained support from numerous international groups, and is therefore credited with playing a role in bringing about the decline of the military regime. Mothers of the Plaza de Mayo still exists today.

Similar movements emerged in Chile in response to the Pinochet dictatorship, including the Association of Relatives of the Detained and Disappeared, an organization much like the Mothers of the Plaza de Mayo.

One of the well-known women of Latin America is the 1992 Nobel Peace Prize winner, Rigoberta Menchú. Her history is told in the autobiographical book *I, Rigoberta Menchú: An Indian Woman in Guatemala*. Menchú was awarded the Nobel Prize for her role in bringing to international attention the atrocities committed against indigenous peoples of Guatemala by the military dictatorship. Menchú's activism is credited with bringing international criticism to the crisis in Guatemala, which helped lead to the peace process. Menchú deals not only with the political system but also with the fight for indigenous peoples to demand recognition of their values, land rights, and cultural systems.

While women's protests against authoritarian regimes have been the most visible examples of "social motherhood," there have been instances where activism has been motivated by familial concern. Amazon Sisters is a group of Brazilian women that was created to stop the development of the Amazon by foreign companies in order to preserve their land and a quality of life for their families. These women staged demonstrations to protest the medical problems and evictions resulting from the destruction of the rain forest and the exploitation of workers.

Ecological concerns were part of the political platform of Benedita da Silva. A Brazilian slum dweller herself, da Silva was elected to the Brazilian congress in 1986 and 1990. The first black woman to be elected, she emphasized the plight of the working poor in Rio de Janeiro's slums. Her 1990 campaign focused on environmental issues relating to workers, living conditions, and abuse of children.

Another example of a black woman in Brazilian politics is Marina Silva. She was born in the state of Acre, located in northwestern Brazil in the Amazon region. As one of 11 children from a poor family, Silva was illiterate until she was 16 years old. As a teenager, she was taken in by nuns and learned to read in the convent. After leaving the convent, she worked as a domestic. Marina graduated from the Federal University of Acre with a degree in history and began her political career along with Chico Mendes, an environmentalist who was assassinated in 1988. She was elected to the federal senate in 1994. As a native Amazonian and senator, Marina built support for environmental protection. In 2003 President Lula appointed her to the position of Environment Minister. Silva was a candidate for the presidency in 2010 and 2014.

A girl in the Peace Community of San José de Apartadó, Colombia. *(Paul Jeffrey)*

Profiles

Selito

Selito was born in Minas Gerais in Brazil and, when he was two years old, moved with his family to São Paulo. During his childhood in the 1960s he used to play in the streets all the time, playing ball games with children of different ages, "…and the drumbeat took place by the side of the field." He learned to play the drums at parties and in the close contact moments of community gatherings. "In my most remote memories, there's always some of the "batucada" drumbeat.

"When I was nine years old, I used to play the *atabaque*, a kind of hand drum, in the *terreiro* (a religious community with African origins) with my siblings. I remember that, by that age, my friends and I liked those games of playing the macumba (a rhythm that is connected to the African original religions) and sing samba."

Selito always makes a distinction between samba as a musical genre and as a cultural trait. "In samba as a musical genre, anyone who can play music and sings can be considered a samba musician. But I understand samba as a culture—a set of practices that rules a group of individuals." And it's in the culture that comes from samba that Selito finds his roots, "…in black culture. In general, under the African philosophical universe from where we come, there is no profane and sacred. As a matter of fact, in life, everything is sacred."

Projeto Nosso Samba (Our Samba Project), where Selito participates, was formed in 1998, with a group of friends, with the objective of creating a space for the propagation, preservation, and sharing of black culture. Each meeting is carefully prepared, with the right choice of the songs to be presented—for them, it is important to know the context in which a song was composed and debated. The project tries to offer an alternative to a national movement in which samba became a profit-driven medium, depriving the most traditional drumbeats of their unique characteristics.

All of the members of the project have other professional activities. Selito works at the Universidade de São Paulo (USP), a public university in São Paulo, as a technician in the College of Geography, helping with research and organizing debates and events.

Anivaldo Padilha

At the time of the military regime in Brazil, Anivaldo Padilha and his fellow prisoners tried to sing to give strength to anyone who was called to be tortured. "I still get emotional today," he says. "The most difficult period in my life was in prison." Born in 1942 in São Pedro da União, a small town in southern Minas Gerais, a state in southeastern Brazil, Anivaldo came to São Paulo when he was five years old.

In the Methodist Church community, he could associate and share with all of society's most excluded sectors. He liked to attend the groups that divided into ages, where they would discuss issues. It was an incentive for reading, a time for questioning, discussing, practicing freedom of thought, discipline in the studies, and discussion in a democratic venue. As a teenager he started to write for the church's newspaper, a kind of an informative bulletin; he also collaborated with other church publications addressed to youngsters and teenagers.

At 17, he joined the old Partido Socialista Brasileiro (Brazilian Socialist Party, PSB) and was part of the church's youth movement. In 1966, Anivaldo started studying social science at Universidade de São Paulo (USP), a public and free university in São Paulo. In 1962 he became a member of Ação Popular (Popular Action), a political organization that at that time was strongly opposed to the military dictatorship. The same year, he became a secretary of União Latino-Americana de Juventude Ecumênica (Latin American Ecumenical Youth Organization, ULAJE).

Despite taking all the necessary precautions at that time—not meeting in public, using a fake name—he and a colleague from Ação Popular, as well as two other friends, were arrested in 1970 after they were denounced by a bishop from the church. Then the torturing began with the objective of finding out to which movement he belonged and the names of other friends. He was afraid of being tortured and of speaking. He went into a deep crisis, and since he was at the mercy of the torturers, he could not find a way out. "I couldn't cooperate. I couldn't do that. It was a non-life life. The only alternative was suicide. I found myself at 29 facing up to the real possibility of dying."

However, not even suicide was possible. There weren't sharp objects, belts, or ropes in the cell. Certain that he would die and fearing collaboration brought Anivaldo into a process of introspection. "I started to think about my life. I thought about the life of Jesus, who, in his story, faced the powers that oppressed the people, and kept walking by the side of the most excluded population. I thought I was there not for a merely political option, but for the involvement motivated by my faith." Then, he realized he had dedicated his life to God and they didn't have the right to take it away. He started to think, then, about his strength before his torturers. "If they need so many to torture me, that's because I'm morally stronger."

Torture, besides causing physical pain, demoralizes, it denies the human condition to human beings. "You search for strength as far as you are tested in your fragility." At that moment, he felt deep serenity, the acceptance of death as something inevitable. "I didn't surrender, but I went into a moment of serenity. This is the path I have to cross; I know why I am here. It's because of choices I made in the past." He fell asleep, and when he woke up, he had gone into a process of amnesia: "I couldn't remember anybody's name. This

is a problem I still have today. They tortured me for all the time they wanted, and I couldn't remember any name. At that time, I felt something had happened to me and erased the names from my memory."

After he was in prison, he had to go into exile, and was unable to say goodbye to his girlfriend. "I had to leave the country before talking to my girlfriend, who was three or four months pregnant. I only could see my son in 1979. As painful as the dictatorship was, it was worse not to live together with my son, Alexandre Padilha,"* he said.

According to Anivaldo, overcoming the trauma was difficult. "The only way to win the torturers, those monsters, was through forgiveness. From that moment on, the nightmares stopped. It was a therapeutic process; it was a way to free myself from the violence of dictatorship one more time."

Anivaldo has already searched for an explanation about that phenomenon of amnesia, but "…for me, the most important thing was that, at that moment, I was going through a mystical experience. I didn't have any doubt about that. It was such a deep experience that there isn't a rational thought that accounts for it."

About faith and religion, Anivaldo asserts, "Faith cannot be perceived as something magical. Faith is something you have inside, which moves you and gives a meaning to your life. It doesn't need to be religious. When you are in a difficult situation, totally and absolutely vulnerable, you have to find strength within yourself. Faith doesn't originate in the emptiness." Anivaldo continues, "At the same time, when evil appears in an absolute way, you can only oppose it as you wake or relive the good you have internally. This good is sublime and sacred. Independently of being religious, God doesn't ask permission to manifest. Because we can't explain such a deep thing, we name it God."

Today, Anivaldo coordinates a work group for the National Truth Commission, which studies the action of churches during the military dictatorship (1964–1985). The Commission has seven members, appointed by President Dilma Rousseff, and serves in different work groups. He coordinates one of them, which investigates the role of church during the military dictatorship. He turns his energy toward investigations by contacting people for declarations, readings, and scheduling of public hearings. His work routine involves collecting declarations from the victims of the dictatorship, and issues in the national and international ecumenical world.

He's a night owl. He likes to be awake until two and three in the morning, and he is "in the shower every day at 8:00 a.m." He likes to have his breakfast with his wife, so that they can talk about what happened the day before and plan the day, sharing the house and housework chores, since they take care of everything by themselves. At 9:00 a.m., he sits in front of his computer and starts his e-mail reading routine, in a number of around 300 a day. He also checks Facebook, which is the channel he uses to disclose information, usually about human rights. He keeps afternoons for meetings and interviews, and he travels regularly to public hearings he carefully plans. It is an intense web of political activism work.

On Sunday mornings, he goes to church "to see friends, fraternize and talk." He thinks the meetings in church offer some contact with different people, a more heterogeneous public who is down-to-earth: "I like to see what kind of opinion is being built, and I end up demolishing thoughts. I like to provoke people to question everything. I give information, ask questions, and try to help them question themselves."

* Alexandre Padilha is a former minister of health in Brazil.

(Paul Jeffrey)

In Embarcación, Argentina, a Wichí indigenous boy aims his slingshot. *(Paul Jeffrey)*

Endnotes

1. "Arte pré-colombiana," *Enciclopédia Itaú Cultural*, accessed October 25, 2014, www.itaucultural.org.br/aplicexternas/enciclopedia_ic/index.cfm?fuseaction=termos_texto&cd_verbete=907&lst_palavras=&cd_idioma=28555&cd_item=8.

2. Dawn Ades, *Arte na América Latina* (São Paulo: Cosac Naify, 1997), 35.

3. Ibid.

4. Leslie Bethell and Mary Amazonas Leite de Barros (trans.), *História da América Latina: América Latina Colonial*, vol. 2. (São Paulo: Universidade de São Paulo, 1984): 644.

5. Ibid.

6. Ades, *Arte na América Latina*, 125.

7. Ibid.

8. Ibid.

9. José Jorge de Carvalho, "Conhecimentos tradicionais no Brasil e na América Latina: uma agenda de resistência e criatividade," www2.cultura.gov.br.

10. Ibid.

11. "Chulucanas Potery History," *Ceramica Chulucanas*, accessed October 25, 2014, www.cotlear.com/History.htm.

12. "Handcrafted Textiles Made in South America," *Inkkas*, last modified December 22, 2012, www.inkkas.com/blogs/blog/7078508-handcrafted-textiles-made-in-south-america.

13. "About the Tarahumara Indians," *Singing Shaman Traders*, accessed October 25, 2014, www.singingshamantraders.com/about-tarahumara.htm.

14. "Yanomamo Indians," *Indian Cultures by Hands around the World*, accessed October 25, 2014, www.indian-cultures.com/cultures/yanomamo-indians.

15. "América Latina," *El Rincón del Vago*, 2002, html.rincondelvago.com/america-latina_1.html.

16. "Conheça as principais danças da América Latina," *Dançando com os países da América Latina*, dancasdaamericalatina.blogspot.com/2008/10/suriname-guiana-granada-barbados-no-tem.html.

17. Sua Pequisa, "Samba e História do Samba," *Sua Pesquisa*, accessed October 20, 2014, www.suapesquisa.com/samba.

18. "Música e Resistência," *Estudio Next*, accessed October 20, 2014, estudionext.com.br/musica-e-resistencia.

19. Lisa Zimmerman, "Women in Latin America," *Latin America Resource Center*, accessed October 20, 2014, stonecenter.tulane.edu/uploads/Women_in_Latin_America_updated-1352754376.pdf.

20. Ibid.

21. Ibid.

22. Ibid.

Arcadia Ventura makes tortillas at her home in San Jose la Frontera, a small Mam-speaking Maya village in Comitancillo, Guatemala. *(Paul Jeffrey)*

Responsively Yours

I Chose Spanish

iStockphoto/power of forever

How do you see the work of God in your life? Sometimes it is in seemingly small choices.

I remember very clearly sitting in my sixth grade classroom in one of those old buildings

Calendar

15 Celebrate **National Hispanic Heritage Month** through Oct. 15. Learn more about the people, histories, culture and contributions at aarp.org/hispanicheritage.

In some ways, this sort of choice—weighing the expected against something that might be useful—is the kind of choice God presents us over and over again. This particular choice didn't involve any great sacrifice or courage on my part, but it was a moment to think beyond the expected pattern and to make a choice for the "useful" alternative.

I suspect that as United Methodist Women members and leaders we have this kind of choice-making opportunity on a regular basis. The decisions we're making may not be monumental ones with earth-shattering consequences, but we often get the chance to question the expected plan and consider other creative ways to engage mission and carry out the Purpose. In fact, we might want to make it a point to question assumptions about planned actions that will have a significant impact. Let's state the assumptions out loud so that we can examine them. Are they still true? Do we expect them to lead to the outcomes that we've said are important? What other values or aspirations should lay alongside the expected course of action for perspective?

While our disciplined study and our intentional listening prepare our hearts to respond to the call of God to participate in God's work in the world, sometimes it seems that small moments of clarity pop up in unexpected areas, and we can only see the impact of the choices we make in those moments in hindsight. God bless you as you recognize those moments and see new possibilities for United Methodist Women to be useful in God's work. ■

HARRIETT JANE OLSON
General Secretary
United Methodist Women
holson@unitedmethodistwomen.org

> Let's state the assumptions out loud so that we can examine them. Are they still true? Do we expect them to lead to the outcomes that we've said are important? What other values or aspirations should lay alongside the expected course of action for perspective?

How To Use This Issue

by **TARA BARNES**

Easter is coming, but now we are in Lent. Next month we will celebrate; this month we mourn, we pray, we fast, we prepare. We listen for God's call and ready ourselves to answer it. For Jesus will rise from the dead and we will become Easter people. Easter comes every year.

Jesus will rise from the dead. Even for a man known to perform miracles his resurrection is surprising. In 1 Corinthians 15, the apostle Paul discusses the resurrection and what it means for followers of Jesus. Read this chapter of the Bible. Discuss it with others or reflect on in individually. United Methodist Discipleship Ministries in partnership with United Methodist Communications produce a Web video series called *Chuck Knows Church*, describing beliefs and practices of The United Methodist Church. This month watch "Chuck Knows Church: Resurrection," which can be found at www.umc.org/news -and-media/chuck-knows-church-resurrection.

If you were given the opportunity to preach a modern-day Sermon on the Mount, what would your sermon entail? What is the good news you would share with a crowd of gatherers to-

day? What does happiness in God mean?

"To offer abundant life, human flourishing, is God's vocation," says Glory Dharmaraj in "A Spirituality Called Happiness," this month's Bible study on pages 8-11. This month, take some time to focus on what would really make you happy.

March is also Women's History Month. United Methodist Women members honor our foremothers and the contributions of women whose bravery, prophecy and action allow us to take for granted the rights we enjoy today by continuing to work for gender equality.

The section introductions in this issue feature women pertinent to United Methodist Women history. Share these women's stories with others. Make a bulletin insert or table centerpieces for your next United Methodist Wo-

men meal, gathering or event. Single issues of this magazine can be purchased through our e-store at www..united methodistwomen.org. Maybe this month's mission for your United Methodist Women group can be to purchase this issue for congregation members. Reading and sharing **response** is being in mission. **response** is the story of you.

Sharing our stories is key to putting our faith, hope and love into action. It's how you connect to the person sitting next to you or praying with you from the other side of the world. In "Yes, You Can Share Your Mission Story" on pages 18-20 Deaconess Amanda Mountain offers practical tips for you to do just that. Jesus, after all, did not give us a user manual but instead shared stories. His parables make us think, and they make us act, and now we are called to motivate others in the same way with our stories. This month, be intentional about trying to connect someone new to United Methodist Women through storytelling (and maybe sharing response). **r**

Tara Barnes is managing editor of **response**.

the **r** list | march

March is Women's History Month

1843

Isabella Baumfree, born into slavery in New York in 1797, changes her name to Sojourner Truth, saying, "The Spirit calls me, and I must go." She begins traveling and preaching to end slavery.

1869

March 23, 1869, Methodist women meet in Boston, Massachusetts, to organize for mission focused on the needs of women and children.

1911

The first International Women's Day was March 19, 1911. It was changed to March 8 in 1913.

1920

The 19th Amendment to the U.S. Constitution giving women the right to vote is ratified August 18, 1920.

63.7%

Women who reported voting in the 2012 presidential elections.

Chapter 5

Faithful People: Religions of the Region

Latin America is a land of great contrasts in its geography, population, and culture. It is also a place of a diversity of faiths and religious expressions. There are Catholics, Protestants, Pentecostals, Buddhists, Muslims, Jews, religions with African roots, and many kinds of spiritual forms in religion and worship in Latin America.

As discussed in Chapter 2, the introduction and growth of Christianity and other religions in Latin America are related to the waves of immigration waves during the colonial period.

It is important to also point out that religious expressions in Latin America are historically and culturally rooted. Most of the religions that arrived in the region were greatly influenced by the strong cultures inherent in the area. Even Christianity that germinated in Latin America was influenced by indigenous (*pueblos originarios*) and African traditions.

Roman Catholic Tradition

From 1492 to 1810, the period beginning with colonialism up to the time of independence, Catholicism (i.e. Roman Catholicism) was the predominant religion all over Latin America, but not necessarily in the Caribbean. One of the main reasons it thrived was due to the alliance of the Portuguese and the Spanish kingdoms. Despite facing difficulties, including the harsh living conditions in the colonies, lack of recruits willing to pursue a missionary life, internal division about issues such as the indigenous and slaves and their catechization, and the subordination to the Portuguese and the Spanish crowns, the Catholic Church managed to be the dominate religion for three centuries.

One of the ways the Catholic Church was able to retain dominance was by adapting to the rituals of the indigenous people and turning a blind eye to the religious syncretism of the African slaves and indigenous people. This flexible attitude adapted by the local Catholic priests toward indigenous people and African slaves, mainly in Brazil, was possible due to the distance that separated the priests from Rome.

The predominance of the Roman Catholic faith was sustained in part by syncretism that incorporated various indigenous and African rituals and deities into the Catholic religion. This integration is seen by the worship of Catholic saints and their images, and especially the devotion to the Virgin Mary.

Syncretism: Beliefs and Resistance

Syncretism varies greatly within the historical and social terms as well as the deities and rituals involved, which are strongly influenced by the context. Indigenous and African people in Latin America used syncretism as way to resist a religion that they were forced to adopt. For example, it provided a way for slaves to clandestinely worship an African Candomblé deity without arousing suspicion from their owners.

Religious syncretism is the fusion or a combination of rituals and beliefs of different religions. In Latin America, syncretism has been observed since its early history, initially as a result of the indigenous resistance to the Catholic religion. Later, the African slaves, who were considered by the church to have no souls, practiced syncretism by incorporating their original beliefs into the Catholic rituals.

Although some African slaves were Muslim, most who came from West Africa brought a faith rich with polytheist beliefs and rituals, based on a strong connection with nature and using natural elements, such as water, plants, leaves, and vegetables, as a way to contact the Orishas (deities from their Yoruba pantheon, a culture found in what today is Nigeria and Benin, also known as Nago) who are the connection between humans and God.

They also had rituals that involved dancing and making offerings to the Orishas. The African-originated Candomblé religion has different rituals and practices according to the nation and the region where it had been practiced. Because the African slaves who were brought to Latin America and the United States were from different nations and faiths, the religion they practiced after their arrival was a result of the combination of these different influences. That is how Candomblé Jeje-Nago arose in Brazil, a blend of the Jejes (Togo and Ghana cultures of today) and the Yorubas or Nagos (from Nigeria).

The beliefs and practices of divination and rituals of the African slaves remained strong in places like Brazil, Haiti, and Cuba, where this kind of syncretic religion with African roots is called Santería. In Brazil this faith is called Candomblé. In Brazil, another form of syncretism which developed out of strong elements of Catholicism is called Umbanda.

According to the writer Muniz Sodré, "The deities of the pantheon are African cosmological principles, i.e., the explanation of how and why the man was put in the world. This occurs with Xango, Ogun, and all deities. Each is endowed with explanatory precepts about humans. Exu is seen as dangerous because he brings what is unstable. It is he who carries speech, the foundation of communication, and is also related to sexuality and to the changes, which are considered dangerous."[1]

Similar to the situation of the early Christians in the beginning years of Christianity, it was forbidden for African slaves to practice their own religion during the colonial period in Latin America. Police could persecute slaves who pursued their religions and even those freed after the end of slavery. In order to disguise their faith and rituals, African slaves identified and named their deities (Orishas) after Catholic saints. For example: Yemanja is Our Lady of Conception, Iansa is Saint Barbara, Xango is Saint Jerome, and Oxala is Jesus.

A more tolerant attitude towards Candomblé practices began around 1970, mainly because of the struggle of Black Movements towards religious freedom.

Indigenous people suffered similar repressive measures in the pursuit of their religious practices. Their rituals and traditions were closely tied to their relationship with the elements of nature: the sun and moon cycles, the use of leaves, roots, and seeds. They also have the belief that some people have healing powers and special connection to the forces of nature, the knowledge of the power of plants, seeds, and natural resources. The presence of a *paje*, a person with healing gifts, is common in an indigenous community. This concept was incorporated with the Christian belief in one who performs miracles.

Throughout the centuries indigenous people have developed a "xamanic" medical system based on their cultural, socio-political, and cosmological vision. This set of knowledge and practices was developed over the centuries and taught by one generation to the next generation to promote health, to prevent and cure diseases, to care for pregnancy, and childbirth.[2]

Religious Syncretism Today

It is important to clarify that there are different terms to explain the dialogue or interrelation among religions. According to Afonso Soares from the Methodist University of São Paulo, it is more appropriate when thinking about the colonial period to use the term syncretism rather than contextualization because many of the Orixa, Yodu, or Santería followers as well as followers of other religions with indigenous or African origins, felt like they were Catholic following Catholic rites although they followed other rituals as well. He says, "they accepted Catholic faith (often forced, it's always good to remember) in its original Christian traditions and withdrew from what did not matter much, and in the end they kept intact what they deemed positive and enriching for their own original worldview."[3] It can be considered that they belonged to two religions, which is syncretism, and did not just incorporate it into their culture and religion, which would be considered contextualization.

Syncretism remains alive today and has become such a part of the daily life in Latin America that is hard to find a person who does not know the different types of tealeaves or herbs to help sleep, or a ritual for prosperity to be performed during New Year's Eve. An example of this mix of religious rituals and celebration is the Lavagem do Bonfim (Washing of the Church of Our Lord of Bonfim) that has happened every year since 1754 on the second Thursday of January. The event attracts around one million people in Salvador, Bahia. Our Lord of Bonfim (Senhor do Bonfim) in syncretism is Oxalá, who is the Father of all in the Afro-Brazilian Candomblé.

The origin of the festivity relates to the time when slaves were forced to wash the interior of the church in preparation for the Catholic feast of Our Lord of Bonfim. Over time, the slaves and the free black people who practiced Candomblé began to associate Senhor do Bonfim with the god Oxalá. Since the Catholic Church did not accept Candomblé, the Africans were banned from washing the interior of the church and the ritual was transferred to the stairs. There have been many arguments in regards to the position of the Catholic Church, which tried for years to restrict the Africans from entering the church. Recently, a more ecumenical style has taken place, uniting priests and Candomblé leaders (Maes de Santo, Mothers of Saint) with the same purpose of honoring our Lord.

Lavagem do Bonfim starts with an ecumenical celebration at the Church of Our Mother of Conception, followed by an 8 kilometer parade (5 miles) to Our Lord of Bonfim Church, where the washing of the stairs is performed by the Mothers of Saint, singing in honor to Our Lord of Bonfim. The women wear traditional white costumes, the color of the Oxalá, with long round skirts, turbans, bracelets of multicolored ribbons imprinted with the name of the Bonfim, and large, colorful necklaces. The event is surrounded by Brazilian popular music such as samba, axé, and others.

This kind of syncretism that incorporates African rituals with Catholic and other religious traditions is common in the region and it is manifested in various ways. It does not exclude people and is not a matter of choosing one and leaving the other. For instance, during New Year's Eve there is the ritual to wear white and to go to the shore and offer gifts, such as flowers, to Yemanja, a Candomblé deity of the sea related to the Catholics as Our Mother of Conception; this can be performed by the Catholics without questioning their faith. As a result, the Latin American people have learned to incorporate multiple religious influences into their own reality.

Recent Facts About Catholicism

During the colonization, the integration and convergence of interests between the State and the Church was strong. Although there was not a unique position and there were many forms of resistance among priests, most of the time the Catholic Church provided powerful opening spaces for colonization by catechizing Indians and slaves, inducing them to accept their subordinate condition. At the same time, there were priests like Fray Bartolomé de Las Casas and José de Anchieta who defended indigenous people and slaves.

The relationship between the Church and State has changed greatly over the centuries. During the period of dictatorships and the re-democratization period, between the late 1950s and the 1980s, the involvement of the Catholic Church in progressive and reformation movements increased. Prime examples are the as ecclesial-based communities grounded on liberation theologies, although recently this influence has become more institutionalized.

Research conducted by the Pew Research Center, notes that in 2010 the number of Christians around the world was about two billion people, and half of them were Catholic. Thirty-nine percent of Christians in Latin America are Catholic.[4]

Of these great numbers of Christians, not all of them practice religion, The number of people who do not attend church is significant. Most of them go only to weddings, baptisms, or special holiday services. At the same time, it is possible to find large numbers of people who are faithful Catholics, but also frequent Candomblé and other forms of worship. People are also converting to Evangelical churches (which includes some non-Protestant traditions) as well as historical Protestant churches and from non-Christian traditions.

Other Christian Denominations

During the colonial period, Protestantism was established through the initiatives of European and North American mission agencies and others with the support of native leadership. By the time of the independence movements in the colonies, the influence of Portugal and Spain were decreasing, which stimulated the arrival and development of Protestant ideas and new churches.

After independence, the Catholic Church faced strong political and institutional challenges, and saw its monopoly weakened by the new governments deciding to separate the State and the Church. Many of the leaders of these governments were educated in Europe and influenced by Enlightenment ideas, Freemasonry, and Anglo-Saxon Protestant religions. They were also inspired by the liberal movement that considered the Protestant ideal more compatible with the incipient capitalism and were interested in the development of the Protestant Church in Latin America.

According to Argentine theologian Pablo Deiros, some of Latin America's greatest liberators for independence, such as Simón Bolívar and José de San Martín, who "… in order to develop their dream of progress and independent life were accompanied by

military personnel, scientists, educators and technical people who were Protestant."[5]

Another factor that contributed to the spread of the Protestant Church on the continent was the European migration in the nineteenth century, especially at the end of the century. A great number of businessmen, military personnel, and other professionals arrived in Brazil, Argentina, and Chile. During this period other Christian denominations also came from Europe. The North American missionaries, including the Presbyterians, Baptists, and Methodists, had started to arrive in the region around the second half of the eighteenth century.

Most of the Protestants involved in missionary activities faced a lot of difficulties. As Deiros notes, "One of the most serious problems faced by the first Methodist missionaries in the Caribbean was the opposition from the plantations owners to evangelize and teach slaves. In spite of the opposition, Methodists already had baptized thousands of slaves and had incorporated them into the church. In 1831, when a slave revolt began in Jamaica, this was crushed with ferocity, the missionaries were threatened, imprisoned, and many slaves lost their lives."[6]

Methodist Presence in Latin America

In his book *Protestantism in Latin America* (*Protestantismo en América Latina*), Pablo Deiros included a historical perspective of the presence of Methodism in Latin America. In 1836, beginning with the arrival of missionary Justin Spaulding in Brazil, American Methodists started to come to the region. Spaulding worked in Rio de Janeiro, which was the capital until 1841. Beginning in 1867, Junius E. Newman and other missionaries who came to Brazil started to consolidate the organization with the first Conference that took place in 1886.[7]

In Uruguay, the mission started in 1835 with missionary Fountain E. Pitts, who organized several meetings to spread the Methodist doctrine. After two years, the mission started to hold services in English, since the

Johnny Antesano, a four-year-old Guarani indigenous boy in Choroquepiao, a small village in the Chaco region of Bolivia, helps his mother, Yela Vilera, in the family garden. With assistance from Church World Service, Antesano's family and their neighbors started their gardens to supplement their corn-based diet with nutritious vegetables and fruits. *(Paul Jeffrey)*

congregation consisted mainly of foreigners. Financial problems forced the end of the mission, which was later resumed in 1867 with John Thomson, who began to preach in Spanish. The Methodist Church was formally organized in 1878 and founded the Crandon Institute, a high school in Montevideo that is still in operation today. More than 135 years later, the Crandon Institute maintains its Methodist ties and is one of the country's most prestigious schools.

The first Methodist Church in Argentina was built in 1843 and has grown steadily preaching in Spanish since its very beginning. A group of Methodist women from the United States started a school in Rosario, which was the foundation for Universidad del Centro Educativo Latinoamericano (University of Latin American Education Center). Colegio Ward (Ward High School) was established in 1913, in Buenos Aires with the support of the Board of Foreign Missions of the Methodist Episcopal Church and the local Methodist Church.

Around 1880, the Methodist Church experienced a strong growth in membership and also of ordained pastors. During the same period, as a result of this growth, it was possible to extend their missions to other countries in Latin America such as Peru, Bolivia, Venezuela, and Ecuador. According to Deiros, the pioneers who spread Protestantism in these countries were Methodist missionaries such as William Taylor, J.G. Price, and Francisco Pezzoti (Ecuador).[8]

In Mexico, the beginning of the Methodist Church can be traced to 1873 with the work of the Methodist Episcopal Church South. "The Methodist Episcopal Church followed in 1873, sending missionaries to explore possibilities and establish congregations. In 1930 Methodism in Mexico became united and the Methodist Church in Mexico was born as an autonomous church. Its bishops are elected every four years. At present the church has six episcopal areas covering 28 of the 30 states of the nation and the federal district."[9]

The Methodist work in Chile began in 1877 along the Pacific coast with William Taylor. By 1888, with the help of Juan Bautista Canut de Bon (1846–1896), a former Spanish Catholic Jesuit who converted to Methodism, the mission in Chile witnessed a revival and had great success, thanks to Canut de Bon who began preaching and evangelizing in Spanish. According to Deiros, from this time on all the Protestants in Chile were referred to as "canutos."[10]

In Puerto Rico, the Methodists began working in March of 1900, when the missionary Charles W. Ores came to the island. From the beginning the work was oriented to education. In 1901 he began a school in San Juan, and afterwards he founded an orphanage for girls.[11]

Recent Religions Movements

Currently, Latin America is seeing growth in Pentecostal and Evangelical churches. In Argentina and Brazil, the rate of increase is impressive: "In 1895, in Argentina, evangelicals amounted to 0.7% of the population, that number rose to 2.6% in 1960, to 5% in 1985, and today is around 8%. In Brazil, the number of evangelicals reached 1% of the population in 1900, 3% in 1950, 6.6% in 1980, 9% in 1991, and 15.4% in 2000, and in 2010 the number of evangelicals reached 42.3 million or 22.2% of Brazilians."[12]

These figures include all non-Catholic Christian denominations that have used the terms Protestant or historical protestant churches. Nowadays, the term evangelical is applied to all non-Catholic churches, including the historical Christian denominations as well as the more recently established ones.

In Latin America there are the religions with an emphasis in "spiritualist beliefs," such as the Espiritas, who believe in reincarnation. In addition, there are traditional Catholics, Protestants, Pentecostals, Buddhists, Muslims, Jews, and many kinds of Spiritualists forms of religion and worship.

A Faith Opened to the Poor

Liberation theology is a movement that started in Latin America to address and answer the historical inequalities faced by Latin American people. The 1950s and 1960s was a period that began with union movements, people organizing in urban centers, and the start of the ecclesiastical-based communities (CEBs), small grass-roots communities of Christian lay people that started with the Catholics in Brazil. Soon CEBs became a model adopted by many other Christian denominations all over Latin America. During the period of dictatorship, the CEBs were the foundation for the surge of social organizations, local leaders, and a strong focus of popular resistance and organization.

The beginning of liberation theology is associated with the release of the book *Teología de la liberación: Perspectivas* (*Liberation Theology: Perspectives*) by the Peruvian priest Gustavo Gutiérrez. The same year, Leonardo Boff, a Brazilian theologian, was publishing articles that became part of the book *Jesus Cristo Libertador* (*Jesus Christ Liberator*). Both theologians had the same perspective that led them to interpret the biblical text as the freedom of the poor. During the 40th celebration of liberation theology, Boff affirmed: "We were with the same Spirit. Since then three generations of theologians inspired by the liberation theology have emerged. Today it is taught in all the continents and embodies a different way of doing theology, from the wretched of the earth to all the corners of the world."[13]

Liberation theology is an attempt to interpret Scripture from the perspective of the poor. It invites us to read and experience the Bible from the plight of the poor. In this way, it is a movement that tries to answer and help poor and oppressed people to overcome their social and economic inequalities and suffering to realize a full life as human beings and children of God. It is a way to take Jesus's life as an example of an option for the poor.

For Leonardo Boff:

> We only properly understand the theology of liberation if one looks beyond the ecclesial and to

the space within the larger historical movement that swept Western societies at the end of the 1960s during the last century. A call for freedom and liberation spoke to young Europeans, afterwards North Americans, and finally the Latin Americans. All aspects of the culture, politics, and daily life habit patterns considered oppressive started to be demolished. As the churches are with the world, this weltgeist took a great number of members with them. They brought into the churches such longings for liberation. They began to ask themselves: What contribution can we Christians give from the specific premises of the Christian faith, from the message of Jesus that has been proved, according to the Gospels, a liberator message? This question was posed by Christians who already took part in the popular media and in the political life that wanted the transformation of society.[14]

According to Boff, liberation theology involves some methodological steps that can be explained as follows:

1. A spiritual encounter, that can be understood as an experience of Christ crucified suffering with the crucified
2. An ethical outrage (indignation), which condemns and rejects an inhumane situation and calls for action to overcome it
3. An observation that includes a structured analysis of the mechanisms that create poverty and oppression
4. A critical judgment through the eyes of faith and reason about the kind of society we have, marked by so many inequities and urgency and ways to overcome them
5. An effective action that effectively advances the process of liberation from the oppressed
6. A collective celebration of victories achieved[15]

The ecumenical movement has been strong in the Latin American Roman Catholic Church but also spread out to other Christian denominations. There was an ecumenical movement in Latin America that developed the liberation theology as well. The Methodist ministries were also involved with liberation theology as it connects with the social actions and justice of the Methodist Church.

During the 1960s, 1970s, and 1980s, there were cases of priests and lay leaders who became involved in political issues, unions, and movements of revolution and resistance to dictatorships that spread over Latin America. One example of this was Anivaldo Padilha, a lay Methodist whose profile is found in Chapter 4. The Methodist leader who worked in ecumenical movements was arrested and tortured during the Brazilian dictatorship period in 1970, with no further charges other than "subversive infiltration in the Methodist Church." After his release, he spent thirteen years in exile.

Most of the religious people who adopted liberation theology were criticized as leaning toward Marxism, and that was one of the main reasons that the movement was not uniform in the Roman Catholic Church. Pope John Paul II was a severe critic of the movement and also punished some of the leaders, including Leonardo Boff and Gustavo Gutiérrez who were sentenced by the Roman Catholic Church to silence. Pope John Paul II stated that the Church should remain with the religious work and he was against political and social justice actions, although he held that the church should stay as a support to the poor.

Liberation theology found fertile soil in other Christian denominations, mostly those with a strong history of social work, such as Methodists, Presbyterians, and others. In the Catholic Church a revival of liberation theology is anticipated following the election of Pope Francis I, who has a history of work with the poor and has been asking the Church to return to its social action roots. There is also a hope that in this period there would be a expanding of the relation with other faith denominations towards a more ecumenical understanding.

Methodist Church in Latin America

Methodism in Latin America developed from British and North American Methodism and most recently and selectively from other European and Korean Methodist mission efforts. Methodism in Latin America was an active part of the uniting movement of the early 1900s. Consequently, Methodist work in some countries was ceded to other denominations as part of mission comity arrangements. Today, Methodism is present all over the region with the exception of French Guyana. In the 1930s the Brazil and Mexico Methodist churches became autonomous. All others became autonomous in the 1970s. There are newly established Methodist Churches in the central and the northern regions of South America. The United Methodist Church continues to exist in Honduras.[16]

British background: The Methodist Church in the Caribbean and the Americas was the first Methodist Church in the Americas before The United Methodist Church. MCCA covers approximately 25 countries, predominantly in English-speaking countries but also in Spanish-, French-, Creole- and Dutch-speaking countries. MCCA has eight Districts (i.e., Annual Conferences). Other Methodist churches, or former Methodist churches with some British influence are located in the Dominican Republic. The oldest Methodist community is in Antigua.

Four Methodist churches have a concordant with The United Methodist Church: Mexico, Puerto Rico, MCCA, and the British Methodist Church.

North American background: The United Methodist Church or its predecessor denominations have been active in Latin America and the Caribbean since the early 1800s. Its work is spread throughout 11 countries: Argentina, Bolivia, Brazil, Chile, Costa Rica, Cuba, Mexico, Panama, Peru, Puerto Rico, and Uruguay. New mission initiatives continue to be launched. These include initiatives in five other countries: Colombia, El Salvador, Honduras (a United Methodist Mission), Nicaragua, and Venezuela. Ecuador and the Dominican Republic are churches in transition from the union movement of the early 1900s. In Guatemala, the Methodist Church was formerly governed by the Primitive Methodist Church in the U.S.A. but is now a national church. Since 1973 it became the Evangelical National Methodist Primitive Church of Guatemala and has a predominantly indigenous membership.

CIEMAL

In 1969, in Santiago, Chile, the Council of Evangelical Methodist Churches for Latin America and Caribbean (CIEMAL) was founded with the purpose of expressing the unity and witness of connectional Methodist churches in the service life and common actions in Latin American and Caribbean countries.

According to the Brazilian Methodist website, the Methodist Church in Latin America has today approximately 215,000, and its mission is realized through congregations located in all major cities, rural and indigenous areas, and slums, with educational programs and services from infancy to youth and old age.[17] Methodists have also created schools, universities, clinics, hospitals, and projects for children who live in the street, women's care, and other forms of social and evangelical service.

CIEMAL binds together Methodist churches of nineteen nations and regions of Latin America and the Caribbean in vital relationships of mutual support, mission, and service. CIEMAL supports life and mission of Methodism within a broad ecumenical Christian context. While affirming the rich heritage of the past and the creative new connections with partners of United Methodist, Methodist, and ecumenical traditions throughout the world, through CIEMAL fresh visions and bold initiatives of witness and mission are emerging for more than 1,400,000 of the people called "Methodist" within this vast region.

For the first time CIEMAL, at the 10th General Assembly in 2013, elected a woman as their president. Rvda. Lizzette Gabriel Montalvo from the Methodist Church of Puerto Rico will lead CIEMAL for the term of 2013–2018.[18]

Ecumenical Approach

Latin America has been a place with strong cooperation among Christians of different denominations and other religions. One of the main ecumenical organizations in the region is the Consejo Latinoamericano de Iglesias (Latin American Council of Churches, CLAI.) The Council is an organization of Christian churches and movements that was founded in 1982. CLAI has a membership of 175 Latin American churches with presence in every country in the region. For CLAI, ecumenism is not an option, but it is a gospel mandate. As in the Gospel of John, "that they may all be one. As you, Father, are in me and I am in you, may they also be in us, so that the world may believe that you have sent me" (John 17:21). In order to follow this, CLAI has the following objectives:

- Promote the unity of God's people as part of the concept of mission and service to the world.
- Support their member churches in their evangelistic work.
- Strengthen capacity and advocacy, also public, social, and political participation of the churches, and of CLAI itself.
- Promote reflection and theological dialogue.
- Train leadership on social issues and pastoral work.[19]

Members of CLAI include more than 150 Baptist, Congregational, Episcopalian, and Evangelical churches together with Lutheran, Moravian, Mennonite, Methodist, Nazarene, Orthodox, Pentecostal, Presbyterian, Reformed, and Waldensian Christians and specialized agencies for youth ministry, theological education, and Christian education in 20 countries of Latin America and the Caribbean.

Confederation of Methodist Women in Latin America and the Caribbean

Methodist Women has a history of organizing in Latin America and the Caribbean. One example of this women's leadership was the Confederación de Mujeres Metodistas de América Latina y el Caribe (Confederation of Methodist Women in Latin America and the

As a member of a women's cooperative, a woman makes jewelry in El Bonete, a small village in northwestern Nicaragua. *(Paul Jeffrey)*

Caribbean) that was established in 1928 with the theme of "United in Spirit, Service and Testimony." This Confederation is linked with the Federations of Methodist Women in Latin America and the Caribbean, which worked to spread Christianity and missionary service in the region. These two regions of the World Federation are defined by language: Latin America and the Caribbean where Spanish and Portuguese is spoken, and North America and the Caribbean where English is spoken. The Federations that are members of the Confederation of Methodist Women in Latin America and the Caribbean are:

- Argentina
- Bolivia
- Brazil (with eight Regional Federations)
- Chile
- Costa Rica
- Cuba
- Dominican Republic
- Ecuador
- Guatemala
- Mexico (with six Regional Federations)
- Nicaragua
- Panama
- Paraguay
- Uruguay

Sympathizer Federations
- Colombia
- El Salvador
- Honduras

As a Methodist women's organization, the Confederation is committed to improve Christian values in the region and in order to achieve this has the mission to:
- Promote the establishment of God's Kingdom
- Stimulate Christian fellowship among Methodist women from Latin America and Caribbean
- Act as conduit of cooperation between them
- Encourage the formation of new Federations
- Encourage and motivate its members to participate in their programs

The Millennium Development Goals (MDG). This is a statement signed by 189 countries in 2000 under the auspices of the United Nations. Through the Millennium Declaration, the signed countries are committed to increase global efforts to reduce poverty, its causes, and manifestations.

The Millennium Declaration addresses the major issues and challenges facing humanity at the beginning of the new century that was organized to:
- Goal 1: Eradicate extreme poverty and hunger
- Goal 2: Achieve universal primary education
- Goal 3: Promote gender equality and empower women
- Goal 4: Reduce child mortality
- Goal 5: Improve maternal health
- Goal 6: Combat HIV and AIDS, malaria, and other diseases
- Goal 7: Ensure environmental sustainability
- Goal 8: Develop a Global Partnership for Development

For the Confederation of Methodist Women in Latin America and the Caribbean these goals are very similar to the Christian objectives and could be translated to a Christian language as:
- Hope to all who live in poverty and in hunger
- Hope to all students
- Hope in the equality of all
- Hope to all children
- Hope for mothers
- Hope in integrity
- Hope in creation
- Hope to the world

In order to follow how these goals are developing, the World Federation of Methodist and Uniting Church Women have an official standing with the United Nations (the Economic Commission for Latin America and Caribbean, CEPAL). Ivonne Pereira Díaz, from Chile, is the Confederation president elected for the period of 2011 to 2016.[20]

United Methodist Women

United Methodist Women is a faith-based membership organization of laywomen within The United Methodist Church. Members are organized for mission and committed to growing as disciples of Jesus Christ in community with other women and building the lives of women, children, and youth. United Methodist Women has been in mission for more than 145 years. United Methodist Women is specifically charged to support ministry with and advocate for the oppressed and disposed with special attention to the needs of women, children and youth (*The Book of Discipline of The United Methodist Church 2012*, Par. 1319). The national office provides resources and opportunities for members to grow spiritually, develop as leaders and serve to work to improve the lives of women, children, and youth nationally and internationally. United Methodist Women has a strong commitment to women, children, and youth in Latin America and the Caribbean, expressed through the work and relationships of Regional Missionaries and the International Ministries staff.

The intersection of United Methodist Women's Regional Missionaries, national staff, and partners and their programs in Latin America offers a current context to a long relationship. Through the vision of the organization expressed in the work of international ministries, the following criteria apply to all who address the needs of women, children and youth through a partnership with United Methodist Women:

- Leadership and organizational development to strengthen women's voice, experience, and authority in church and society
- Justice through compassionate service and/or advocacy
- Social action in areas such as economic justice, health and health care, and immigrant and civil rights
- Equipping women, children, and youth for transformation through academic and health education, skills training, and economic development

In order to fulfill these objectives, United Methodist Women developed a methodology of work that combines relationships with programming in the following ways:

- *Networking*: The interaction with partners to exchange information, resources and widen contacts with other organizations and leaders who share the priority of working with women, children, and youth.
- *Scholarships*: The offering of educational tuition and cost assistance for women and young adults seeking professional training that will enhance their communities and countries.
- *Grant Partnership*: A partnership that is enhanced by Mission Giving through grants for specified projects that directly impact women, children, and/or youth.
- *Missionary Programming*: An on-the-ground effort by United Methodist Women Regional Missionaries who work with partner organizations and leaders in strengthening the capacity and voice of women, children, and youth.
- *Member Interaction*: The offering of opportunities for United Methodist Women members from the United States to personally connect and interact with partner organizations and members within Latin America and the Caribbean through the Ubuntu Explorer Journeys and Global Justice Volunteers..
- *Leadership Training Events (LTE)*: Training seminars and workshops for women and youth held at national and regional levels and coordinated by the Regional Missionaries and United Methodist staff.
- *Resourcing*: Making it happen by sharing materials that supplement the education, leadership, management, and program work of church and partner organizations.
- *Advocacy*: Public support and solidarity for the work and situations of partner organizations and the women, children, and youth they work with.

The partnerships and programs developed are implemented through the Regional Missionaries of Latin America and the Caribbean, United Methodist Women Initiatives of International Ministries with women, children, and youth, and the funding partnerships that have developed over time through the cross-functional International Ministries' teamwork and relationships. The region has capacity for two Regional Missionaries. Currently, The Reverend Serna Samuel is Regional Missionary and is working with the English- and French-speaking districts of MCCA. A new Regional Missionary will be commissioned for the Spanish- and Portuguese-speaking part of the region.

From 2000 through 2012, Wisdom and Witness was the work of United Methodist Women through former Regional Missionary Rosangela de Oliveira for the Latin American region. The Regional Missionary Initiative is one of the responses of the International Ministries Committee to the recommendations that came out from the 1993 Latin America Working Conference held in Ecuador.

Wisdom and Witness started in 2001 to address the needs of Latin America and the Caribbean in terms of increasing the women's participating in mission through leadership development. The purpose of the program was to promote and support the leadership development of Methodist Women in Latin America and the Caribbean in the mission of justice for women in the church and society.

In this sense, leadership development is a vital element in building and sustaining an inclusive church and just society. Leadership skills are fundamental to empower women to increase their participation in decision-making bodies, to generate the church's solidarity with women's human rights, and to develop the theological voice of women for justice, peace, and equality.[21]

The primary beneficiaries of Wisdom and Witness are Methodist women in Latin America and the Spanish-speaking Caribbean and their organizations. Many of the women who take part of the training are from multi-racial or ethnic backgrounds as well as different cultural backgrounds, and from poor communities and with few years of schooling. The programs objectives are:

- Support and promote leadership training at local, national and regional levels;
- Network with Methodist women's organizations, women in alternative ministries, and women's non-governmental organizations;
- Raise awareness of women's human rights and the multiple forms of discrimination against women

From 2001 through 2012, Wisdom and Witness primarily worked on building the relationship of United Methodist with Methodist women's organizations in the region. The network was extended to women at ecumenical organizations and other denominations through gender training in partnership with Universidad Bíblica Latinoamericana (UBL) in Costa Rica. This initiative was held for four years. The gender manual, *Gender and the Church*, created by International Ministries, was translated into Spanish and Portuguese and has been used by Protestant, Pentecostal, and Catholic women. Other ecumenical organizations have introduced the gender manual at their own leadership training sessions, as well.

All the educational and leadership opportunities were developed in partnership with United Methodist Women and ecumenical women's organization. Educational resources have been produced for women and youth to engage in mission. New opportunities have been offered to Methodist women and young women to experience the challenges of women's human rights communities at global events such as the World Social Forum on two occasions and at United Nations Conferences.

Simultaneously, the retired Regional Missionary Doreen Boyd conducted this work in the English- and French-speaking Caribbean. As part of its outreach program to church leaders of the Methodist Church in the Caribbean and the Americas (MCCA), a series of gender awareness and leadership training workshops for women and men of MCCA titled "Transforming Relationships Between Women and Men in the Church and Society" were developed. These workshops were specifically geared for participants from all districts of MCCA and were implemented in each one except Haiti.

Recently, the work of International Ministries with women, children, and youth in Latin America and the Caribbean continues to focus on empowering women and youth through leadership training, networking, and advocacy of women's human rights to increase participation of women and youth in the mission of the church and society. All programming and network activities are facilitated by the region's Regional Missionary and reflect the needs and priorities of the communities she serves. The plan is to continue to:

- Build relationships with Methodist, United Methodist, ecumenical, and grassroots programs
- Work on projects and initiatives that focus on issues of health (particularly primary health care and HIV/AIDS), gender equality, and the elimination of violence against women
- Support uprooted and marginalized people.
- Work primarily through training programs, seminars, workshops, strategic planning, and network development
- Reach out to ecumenical partners, especially in the development of resources and women's or youth networks

United Methodist Women's connections to programs, organizations, and advocacy efforts for children, youth, and young adults have been through International Ministries' funding partners and have developed over time through the work of the cross-functional staff team and General Board of Global Ministries missionaries and the Regional Missionaries.

Region-wide Methodist organizations such as CIEMAL and MCCA Youth Organization receive support from International Ministries as do national-level youth desks and programs. Church and grassroots/NGO organizations also connect to United Methodist Women and Global Ministries through grant partnerships. Scholarship recipients also come to United Methodist Women through these church and organizational connections in Latin America. Potentially, as GJV programs that meet the partner's expressed needs and priority issues. United Methodist Women and Global Ministries are connected to church missionaries and NGOs through partnerships.

Action in Haiti

United Methodist Women has worked with women, children, and youth in Haiti for many years prior to the earthquake. Since the January 2010 earthquake in Haiti, United Methodist Women has continued to be committed with the long-term recovery efforts there as the people of Haiti work to rebuild the country and their lives and livelihoods. In the coming year, Serna Samuel, whose responsibility includes Haiti, is working with the Methodist Women's League of Haiti to determine the necessary steps to organize an executive structure for more effective organizational and mission outreach. This work will be in conjunction with the overall MCCA women's organization. She will also continue to work with the women to set priorities among the numerous needs and assist them in determining what their response will be. United Methodist Women has committed around $120,000 towards support for Haiti in the aftermath of the January 2010 earthquake.

Over the past 15 years, the cross-functional International Ministries with women, children, and youth teams has connected with Methodist, ecumenical, and grassroots partner organizations. The partner base has developed cross-functional team members, missionaries, and outreach to International Ministries by Methodist, ecumenical, and grassroots/NGO organizations. All endeavors with partners in the Latin America and Caribbean region work towards greater leadership and organizational capacity for women and youth, supporting justice through compassionate service actions with actual or planned for methods of advocacy to address root causes and social issues, and serve to mutually equip women, children, and youth through education and skills training.

Faith and Mission towards the Future

The history and beliefs of The United Methodist Church helped establish a solid base of social justice in Latin America. Throughout its mission and membership, Methodism has been providing an important service in presenting faith combined with education, health, culture, and social action.

To summarize the reflection on Methodism in Latin America, we turn to Magali do Nascimento Cunha, from the Methodist University of São Paulo, the Faculty of Theology of the Methodist Church and a member of the Committee of the World Council of Churches. In her paper, *Mission and Ecumenical Commitment, Reflections from Latin American Pastoral Context in the XXI Century*, she points out we need to consider that since its beginning, the Christian practices in Latin America were focused on expansionism, proselytism, and conversion.[22]

The action of the church in Latin America was based on the colonizing work of the Spanish and Portuguese on one hand, and on the other, it was highly influenced by the missionary work of the Protestant churches of North America. But in all cases, preaching was focused on conversion. The Protestant church had two requirements: abandonment of the Roman Catholic denomination and assimilation of the way of living brought by church missionaries from the north.

Although some churches have tried to introduce "Latin Americanization," the mission continued to be understood as a conversion project or of building new churches. This tends to create disconnect with the reality of the Latin American population and its context.

More recently, new elements were added to the religious landscape of the region with the increased members of evangelicals, Pentecostals, revivalists, and those of charismatic renewal religions in Latin America. That movement has been considered by many as a phase where religion is labeled as one providing immediate results, one that resolves problems, including the social climbing of its members as a proof of God's blessings.[23]

In that sense, Cunha calls our attention to three points that should be considered when thinking about religious mission in Latin America:

- The mission must be connected with ways that people find to build community life.
- The theological and pastoral approaches need to criticize individualism and consumerism, including their religious expressions.
- It is necessary to see signs of hope and change that come out of the experiences of the poor, who survive and resist the system. For that reason, theological and pastoral reflection need to be connected to the reality of being faithful to the principles of the Gospel.[24]

Thus, the church should seek to achieve a mission connected to the ecumenical commitment involving an intercultural process, which, as Cunha explains, is the process to become aware of the local culture and to respect the agents, the cultural, and social context. For that reason, it is necessary, among other things, to meet and hear the people involved. This requires community life and freedom. Interculturation (to be intercultural), therefore, emphasizes the local situation, takes a look at the local culture, and considers the whole context: socioeconomic, political, religious, and educational. This process should also articulate the local and regional issues with regard to macro-cultural manifestations such as racial, ethnic, and gender issues.

Interculturation is a way to break the insulation produced by an excessive concern with local issues. Communities and groups, therefore, can think locally and act globally. Also, it is necessary for the Church to assume a pastoral role with a public dimension, which "means insertion of the Church in public plural spaces, implying the participation of every Christian as citizen to take the social responsibility of the Church, which

A woman walks home through a cornfield after washing her laundry in a river in Las Flores, Ixcan, Guatemala.

(Paul Jeffrey)

cannot be an isolated body, but a sign of the Kingdom of God."[25]

In this sense, to proclaim the values of the kingdom and God's righteousness it is necessary to go in the opposite direction to all forms of individualism, consumerism, and social exclusion, working on all fronts of human dignity. Besides, it is important to foster the inclusion of people in all dimensions of public life, promoting fellowship among people and communities, avoiding any manifestation of discrimination or exclusion of individuals and groups. These are the fundamental forms of participation in God's mission. The church needs to consolidate more and more as a body, a living organism, and as a community. "The Church needs to be expressed as a living organism, a community of faith, worship, growth, witness, worship, love, support, and service. In this community, women and men are awakened and nourished, grow, share, and live together, express your life and build the body of Christ and are trained for service to people and communities."[26]

The role of the missionaries of the Church, for Cunha, is to make it possible for spaces of community life and mutual support to exist where people can congregate, talk, build on each other, and empower themselves collectively to take action in the world; after all, this is the nature of the Church. She concludes that:

> in a pluralistic continent where both cultural and religious expressions, the ecumenical perspective of respect and appreciation are fundamental to any missionary effort, the ecumenical experience has shown that sharing the gospel does not mean talking about it but living it. And living the Gospel means to signal the kingdom of God, believing that God's Spirit manifests itself in different ways through different channels—it is not only in the Church. In this sense respect and tolerance should revert into concrete attitudes in relation to different cultures of Western hegemonic culture and religious experiences different from the standard set by the Anglo-Saxon Christianity.[27]

In Latin America, religion has an important role to accept people, regardless of their cultures, diversity, social and economic contexts, as an expression of living faith that respects and recognizes the value of human beings as a God's creation.

The Methodist Church and its members have had an important role understanding the need to align with an ecumenical vision bringing together the commitment with the missionary action and the faith. At the same time, it is necessary to recognize that there is a favorable moment towards that understanding by missionaries. Recently there was a reverse movement in Latin America, a movement of more exchange in the experience of mission. In that case, Latin America would not be just a place that receives missionaries, but also a place where receivers, or the "missionized," and missionaries are in a kind of partnership that implies that both groups mutually benefit each other and work toward common goals. In this way, in mission there has always been an implicit partnership with local leadership and missionaries from abroad working side by side with mutual collaboration and the same aims. It is a way to recognize that each partner has something to contribute. As Carlos Cardoza-Orlandi states: "We need to be increasingly aware of the asymmetric in cross-cultural encounters. I …hope that this historical and intercultural awareness may contribute to changing missional practices that have been considered imperialistic, oppressive, paternalistic, and culturally insensitive."[28]

Ursula de Lue weaves a basket in Nahuizalco, El Salvador. *(Paul Jeffrey)*

Profiles

Márcia Quintino

"All of my life, I've said I would work with children," says Márcia, who was born in São Paulo, but lived in Pinhal, a city in the countryside of the state, until she was two years old. Her father used to say he was an atheist, but when he met her mother who was Presbyterian, he opened up to religion and converted to Christianity. When they moved back to São Paulo in the 1960s, "my mother decided to visit the church that was closer to our home, it was a Methodist church. And since then, the family started to worship at that community."

Ever since she was 20 years old, Márcia taught Sunday school to the youth class. One of the Bible studies that "showed the prophets as denouncers of social causes" provoked an intense reaction in her and in her group of students. It was a call for a more practical spirituality.

After failing twice to pass the entrance exam at the School of Medicine, she instead was able to study speech-language pathology and graduated. When she was 26, she already had two children, Luciana and Rafael. At that time, she did not work but was dedicated to the care of her home and family for 14 years.

In 1983, the municipal government offered to the church the administration of a daycare in Jabaquara, a neighborhood in the southern section of São Paulo, next to the Methodist community where Márcia worships. The church accepted the challenge. "My mother became a director, and I used to work as a volunteer, after leaving my kids at school," says Márcia. She started to visit the Associação dos Movimentos de Entidades Sociais Conveniadas (Association of the Convened Movements of Social Organizations, AMESC) and discuss the day care policy, then she became a counselor at this association due to the fact she is Protestant. "It was the first time the fact that I was Protestant was appreciated, and I was very happy for that," she says.

When Márcia's mother became a widow, she came to live with her, and Márcia went back to work. "I missed dedicating myself to something," says Márcia, "but today, I see that being able to be with my children was a great privilege." In the 1990s, she started working at the Bank of Boston, and now she is at Fundação Itaú Social, where she works in social mobilization. "So my dream of working with children came true."

A happy picture? Márcia is proud of the achievements of her son, Rafael, who brilliantly distinguished himself in his profession, and now lives in Canada. And Luciana, her eldest child, who has given her a grandson, also likes what she does. She is a great English teacher.

And, what gives you strength? "The community and faith support me; a group of people on whom I depend. People who understand you and listen to you. If I don't go there some Sundays, I miss it." She likes to have news from everyone, to talk. "There are people in the community with whom I have emotional bonds that are stronger than blood bonds."

Mariana

"My paternal grandmother was one of the strongest persons I ever met. She fought and never gave up during her whole life. She has always been an example of strength to me," says 22 year-old Mariana. She attends the School of Management and has a special interest in oreign trade. She's a fighter, and pays for her studies with the money she earns as an intern at a multinational company. There, she works in the logistics sector; she checks the arrival of equipment produced abroad and traded in Brazil. Happy with her job, Mariana applied to become a permanent staff member and to move forward in her career.

She lives with her mother, brother, and maternal grand-mother in São Paulo. Her days are always rushed, as she wakes up early, works all day long, and goes to the university at night. On weekends, she likes to be with friends and family. What is her favorite entertainment? She loves watching movies. "I always wanted to work in movies, because they are my passion. Movies are a limited trade in Brazil, so I chose an area in which I could have a more stable job. If I have the opportunity to appear on movies in the future, that will be great."

Her passion for movies led her to visit New York, which she knew from films: "I saved some money, dared to do it, and went by myself. It was one of the best experiences in my life. When the plane landed, I thought: 'My God, I can't believe it, I'm making my dream come true!'"

How about the future? She was unhappy at her previous job, and hoped she would be able to do much more. In this new company, she has more opportunities to grow. Since she started working there, she has felt like she had a shot of enthusiasm. Her work is being acknowledged, and this is already a dream coming true: "I want to grow in this company, get to know many places, and travel."

Mariana is Catholic; she was baptized, and although she considers herself religious, she does not attend church. She believes in God but doesn't pray every night. She likes to wear a scapular (a kind of religious necklace), and when she forgets to wear it, she feels unprotected. "And when I'm going through hard times, I ask: 'God, please help me.'"

Vanesa Silva de Soza (left) and Yulimara Machin da Silva, both eight years old, play in the rain in Brazil's Esperança Sustainable Development Project. *(Paul Jeffrey)*

Endnotes

1. "Fé," *A Cord a Cultura*, accessed October 15, 2014, antigo.acordacultura.org.br/mojuba/programa/fé-0.

2. Luciane Ouriques Ferreira, "Apresentação," *Medicina Tradicional Indígena em Contextos* (Ministério da Saúde; Fundação Nacional de Saúde, 2007), 10.

3. Afonso M. Ligorio Soares, "Valor teológico do sincretismo numa perspectiva de teologia pluralista," *Ciberteologia, Revista de Teologia & Cultura*, Ano VI, n. 30, ciberteologia.paulinas.org.br/ciberteologia/wp-content/uploads/downloads/2010/07/03-Sincretismo-e-teologia-pluralista.pdf.

4. "Latin America's Catholics in the Spotlight as Pope Francis Is Installed," *Pew Research Religion & Public Life Project*, last modified March 18, 2013, www.pewforum.org/2013/03/18/latin-americas-catholics-in-the-spotlight-as-pope-francis-is-installed.

5. Pablo Deiros, *Historia del Cristianismo en América Latina* (Buenos Aires: Fraternidad Teologica Latinoamericana, 1992), 677.

6. Ibid., 652.

7. Pablo Deiros, *Protestantismo en América Latina* (Buenos Aires: Editorial Caribe, 1997), 678.

8. Ibid.

9. "Methodist Church of Mexico," *World Council of Churches*, accessed October 27, 2014, www.oikoumene.org/en/member-churches/methodist-church-of-mexico.

10. Deiros, *Protestantismo en América Latina*, 679.

11. Ibid., 681.

12. "Número de evangélicos aumenta 61% em 10 anos, aponta IBGE," *G1 Brasil*, last modified June 29, 2012, g1.globo.com/brasil/noticia/2012/06/numero-de-evangelicos-aumenta-61-em-10-anos-aponta-ibge.html.

13. Leonardo Boff, "Quarenta anos da Teologia da Libertação," *LeonardoBOFF.com*, last modified August 9, 2011, leonardoboff.wordpress.com/2011/08/09/quarenta-anos-da-teologia-da-libertacao.

14. Ibid.

15. Ibid.

16. Deiros, *Protestantismo en América Latina*, 677.

17. José Geraldo Magalhães, "Igreja Metodista tem quase 215 mil membros no Brasil," *Igreja Metodista Portal Nacional*, last modified June 26, 2012, www.metodista.org.br/igreja-metodista-tem-quase-215-mil-membros-no-brasil.

18. "CIEMAL," *General Board of Global Ministries of The United Methodist Church*, gbgm-umc.org/latinam-caribbean/ciemal.html.

19. "Institucional," *Consejo latinoamericano de iglesias*, accessed October 25, 2014, www.claiweb.org/institucional/que_es_clai/queeselclai2.html.

20. "Confederación de Mujeres Metodistas de America Latina y el Caribe – CMMALC," paper, August 18, 2013.

21. "Wisdom and Witness," Carol Van Gorp, executive for international ministries, United Methodist Women National Office.

22. Magali do Nascimento Cunha, "Missão e compromisso ecumênico," *Revista Caminhando*, v.11, nº 17 (Jan./ Jun. 2006): 80–87.

23. Magali do Nascimento Cunha, "Consumo: novo apelo evangélico em tempos de cultura gospel," *Estudos de Religião*, n. 26 (Jun. 2004): 53–80.

24. Ibid.

25. Cunha, "Missão e compromisso ecumênico," 80–87.

26. Ibid.

27. Ibid.

28. Carlos F. Cardoza-Orlandi, *Mission: An Essential Guide* (Nashville: Abingdon Press, 2002), 15.

Eight-year-old Yulimara Machin da Silva in the rain in Brazil's Esperança Sustainable Development Project.

(Paul Jeffrey)

Closing Words

In this book we explored the richness of the pre-Columbian civilizations: how the Incas had the technology to build pyramids; how the Mayan astronomers developed their own calendar, how the Spanish colonizers coveted the Aztecs' treasures, and how the Tupis were linked to nature, taking from the earth their food and resources for healing.

We saw the struggle of the Latin American countries trying to achieve independence, and how the women helped in this process. Also, we learned how difficult it is for the region to stabilize economy and politics in a globalized scenario. We read how centuries of exploitation of land and people created so many inequalities, which cause so many people in the region to suffer from poverty, diseases, violence, and racism, and lack of opportunities to improve themselves. At the same time, how Latin America has not been suffering passively but has tried to overcome in different ways, throughout the centuries, the historical inequalities and injustices.

The culture has been a great expression of resistance in Latin America, and a place where ancient traditions, beliefs, food habits, and ancestral healing wisdom are preserved.

But there is one issue that is present throughout the region, and that is religion. Some places are dominated by different denominations with special characteristics and in accordance with the region.

Latin America is a region where faith and religion have played an important role throughout its history, since pre-Columbian civilization, during the Colonial period, through the independence process and today. The influence of religion endures even today.

Religions and their missionaries have had complex and mixed roles. In some periods in history, they worked to support the established power and government; helped colonizers, politicians or militaries; and oppressed indigenous people, the enslaved, and the vulnerable. In other times, religious people were present to help the poor, the sick, the needy, and to fight against poverty and injustice throughout the region.

We can say that the influence of religion has shaped Latin America and left a mark on the economic, social, and cultural realms. Examples of this are our festivals— Carnival in Brazil, Day of the Dead in Mexico, etc. All of them, in some way, are related to or originated from religious celebrations.

To conclude, I hope that by reading this book you will connect with the people of Latin America, and that it ignites a desire to continue to learn about our land, our culture, and to share our Christian sisterhood. I believe that despite all the diversity in Latin America, it is possible to spread or reinforce the idea of a united region, and that faith could be our bond.

A faith that embraces all and creates a place that is marked by fraternity, solidarity, and shared beliefs, as it is recommended by the ecumenical bodies. So this faith that would be shared with all the brothers and sisters through dialogue and profound respect could be our mission towards the common good of all the people in the world.

Two-year-old Maria Nela Erasto, a Wichí indigenous girl in Santa Victoria Este, Argentina. *(Paul Jeffrey)*

Appendix A

Latin American Movies and Websites

MOVIES

Latin American Women Artists 1915-1995
Directed by Eric Marciano, 1995
According to IMDB reviewer Jane Feyer, "Latin America has produced some of the most innovative, exciting, and relevant artists in the contemporary art world. This film explores the critical and influential role of women artists in Latin America."

Mestizo: Una Historia Del Arte Latinoamericano
Directed by Juan Cruz Sáenz
Available at tal.tv/video/historia-de-la-mujeres-en-latinoamerica.
This video series tells the history of visual arts in Latin America in 13 chapters, from the pre-Columbian era through contemporary times. Reflecting on the inter-relationship between Latin American artists, the influence they exerted in other countries, the social and political contexts that marked their creations, and the impact of their artistic expressions on Latin American identity.

Rigoberta Menchú: Broken Silence
Directed by Félix Zurita, 1992
The movie presents a profile of the 1992 winner of the Nobel Peace Prize, Rigoberta Menchú, whose life has become a symbol of suffering, not only of the Quiche Maya group, but also of the all the indigenous peoples of the Americas.

O Povo Brasileiro
Directed by Isa Grispum Ferraz, 2000
A TV series with 10 chapters based on the book by the same name from the anthropologist Darcy Ribeiro. The TV show, hosted by the author, includes interviews with historians and social scientists, and presents the anthropologist's view about how the Brazilian people were formed.

Kamchatka
Directed by Marcelo Piñeyro, 2002
This is a fictional movie about a family in a rural area trying to hide from oppression during the Argentine dictatorship period of the 1970s.

Missing
Directed by Costa-Gravas, 1982
The movie is based on the true story of Charles Horman, an American journalist, who disappeared in the bloody aftermath of the Chilean coup of 1973 that deposed the democratically elected socialist President Salvador Allende.

The Official Story
Directed by Luis Puenzo, 1985
It tells the dramatic story of a middle-class teacher who discovered that the child she adopted could be a daughter of a *desaparecido*, a political prisoner who was killed during Argentina's last military dictatorship (1976-1983).

Captain Pantoja and the Special Services
Directed by Francisco Lombardi, 2000
Based on the book from Peruvian writer Mario Vargas Llosa, this movie tell the history of an army captain in charge of a special mission to transport a group of prostitutes along the Amazon River.

City of God
Directed by Fernando Meirelles, 2002
Based on the novel with the same name, the movie presents the situations of two boys growing up in the slums of Rio de Janeiro, Brazil, during the 1970s and 1980s.

The Motorcycle Diaries
Directed by Walter Salles, 2004
The movie presents a motorcycle road trip Erenesto "Che" Guevara took through South America in his youth and considered it to be a turning point in his life.

The House of the Spirits
Directed by Bille August, 1993
Based on the novel by Chilean writer Isabel Allende, it tells the story of a family from the perspective of the women, spanning four generations, and reflect the post-colonial political and social upheavals in Chile.

WEBSITES:

Fondo para el Desarrollo de los Pueblos Indígenas de América Latina y El Caribe (The Fund for the Development of Indigenous Peoples of Latin America and the Caribbean)
www.fondoindigena.org/drupal/es/
News, articles, and movies about indigenous people groups in Latin America.

Latin America Virtual Library
www.bvmemorial.fapesp.br
Books, papers and resource materials about Latin America.

ISA – Instituto Socioambiental
(Socio-Environmental Institute)
www.socioambiental.org
Information and news about indigenous peoples in the Amazon region.

CEPAL (Comisión Económica para América Latina y el Caribe) in United Nations Economic Commission for Latin America and the Caribbean (ECLAC)
www.eclac.org
Regional Commission of United Nations for Latin America. It has the aim to work to uplift economic situation in the region.

IADB (Inter-American Development Bank) IDB
www.iadb.org
Database, news, and articles about all the countries in Latin American and the action for development in the region.

Wichí indigenous girls ride a bike in an indigenous neighborhood of Embarcación, Argentina. *(Paul Jeffrey)*

Marisol Sandoval teaches class at an elementary school in the El Escalon neighborhood of Santa Catarina Masahuat, El Salvador. *(Paul Jeffrey)*

Appendix B

United Methodist Women-Supported Projects in Latin America

United Methodist Women Mission Giving supports partners and programs in Latin America and the Caribbean. You can give to these programs via project #3019240 Latin America Programs, a supplementary giving opportunity. United Methodist Women members are encouraged to give through regular giving channels and note the funds are for Latin America Programs. You can also send the check directly to the national office. Please make the check payable to "United Methodist Women" with the project name and number in the memo section.

A list of United Methodist Women partnerships in Latin America includes:

Antigua

*   Gilbert Agricultural and Rural Development Center. Gilbert Agricultural and Rural Development Center/Methodist Church in the Caribbean and the Americas (MCCA). Mercers Creek, Antigua.

Argentina

*   Pastoral for Women. Partner: Argentine Federation of Methodist Women. Training/education to address violence/bullying, addiction, reproductive health and violence against women/girls/teens and families. Service area: Throughout Argentina.

Bolivia

*   Ministry with Children and Teens. Partner: Evangelical Methodist Church in Bolivia. Preparation of Christian education materials that focus on child rights, self-worth, health, and abuse for children and teens in the church. Service area: Throughout Bolivia.
*   Vocational Training of Indigenous Women. Partner: Methodist Women's Federation of Bolivia. Equipping women through vocational training in leadership, business, and agriculture. Service area: Throughout Bolivia.
*   PIM Staff Salary Support. Partner: Women's Desk, Evangelical Methodist Church In Bolivia. Salary support for the Women's Desk Coordinator to develop, implement and train women of Bolivian church. Service area: Throughout Bolivia.

Brazil

*   Tapepora Mission. Work with women, children, and youth. Advocacy training of indigenous members of the Brazil Methodist Church towards self-determination, access to health, care, and freedom of expression within the church. Service area: Aldeia Bororó, Dourados Indian reservation, Dourados-Mato Grosso do Sol in Brazil.
*   Leadership Development. Partner: Confederation of Methodist Youth (the national organization) in Brazil. To equip young people with faith and skills training to empower their futures. Service area: Throughout Brazil.

Caribbean

*   MCCA. Conference for young adults in the church ages 25–45, an age group disappearing from church membership. The aim is to lift up issues that affect participants, equip them to become

actors who transform these conditions and generate a commitment to the Methodist Church as the agent of transformation. Service area: Region Wide.

- MCCA Women and UMW Regional Missionary Serna Samuel. Eliminating Violence against Women and Girls through Policy Formation and Implementation. Project will develop a plan for the MCCA Women's organization to write and advocate for acceptance and implementation towards elimination of violence against women and girls in the MCCA and wider nations of the Caribbean.

Chile

- Strengthening Leadership Capacities of Women to Live Healthy Lives. Partner: Educacion Popular en Salud (EPES). Equipping women to improve their physical and psychological Health through training in the popular education method. Service area: Haulpen of BioBio Region, Chile.
- Project for Fire and Earthquake Affected Women. Partner: Confederation of Latin America and Caribbean Methodist Women, Chile. Project offers skills training in weaving, seafood preparation and pottery to women in the cities of Valparaiso, Arica and Iquique who lost both home and belongings.

Colombia

- Empowering ecumenical women's networks in Colombia. Partner: CEPALC. Strengthening Protestant women's leadership and Organization through workshop training on biblical women leaders, gender and women's rights. Service area: Bogotá, Córdoba, Sucre, Boyacá, Casanare of Colombia.
- Women are Free, Committed and Victorious. Partner: Colombia Methodist Church. Promotion of women's emancipation in church and Society towards acceptance of being created in the image and likeness of God through biblical gender and leadership training. Service area: Costa, Eje Cafetero and Valle Districts.

- Washington Office on Latin America (WOLA). Project: Supporting Afro-descendant women in Colombia through advocacy and advocacy training on human and land rights for all. Service area: Throughout rural Colombia.

Costa Rica

- Women's Economic Development Network. Projects to create a virtual community of women and leadership development for sustainable economic enterprise efforts. Located in San José, Costa Rica, serving Latin America and the Caribbean.
- Women's Economic Development Network. Projects to create microenterprise Leadership Development for small businesswomen to be able to access the tools and information needed to run a sustainable business. Located in San José, Costa Rica, serving Latin America and the Caribbean.

Dominican Republic

- Organización para el Desarrollo de las Mujeres Inmigrantes Haitianas y sus Familiares (ODEMIHF-Organization for the Development of Immigrant Haitian Women and their Families). Addresses women's reproductive and sexual health rights of Haitians living in the Dominican Republic.
- International Child Care and their Dominican Republic Child Care program. Community-based rehabilitation. Project will address the needs of children with disabilities through family training on physical and psychological care as well as the stigma and discrimination faced daily by persons with disabilities.

Ecuador

- 2013 Seminar and Meeting. Partner: United Evangelical Methodist Church of Ecuador The Methodist. Women of the Evangelical Methodist Church of Ecuador held their 2013 meeting in September to celebrate a Bicentennial of Methodist Women and their role in independence, peace, and justice and hold a seminar to make an action plan to address the Millennium Development Goals.

- Association of the Women of the Evangelical United Methodist Church of Ecuador. Women's Training and Empowerment. Project will strengthen the women's association through integrated trainings on spiritual formation, witness and service.

Grenada

- GRENCODA. Youth development skills training program Service area: St. John, St. Mark, and St. Patrick, Grenada.

Guyana

- Methodist Church in the Caribbean and the Americas Women's seminar on spiritual growth, health, gender equality, parenting, disabilities, and gangs. Service area: Georgetown, Guyana.

Haiti

- Agricultural Missions. US-based international organization in Haiti. They partner with Joining Hands Foundation (FONDAMA) on revitalization of Haiti agriculture. The project has a national strategic plan, community–based disaster response preparedness, a youth camp on food sovereignty, the environment, climate change and small scale farming for youth; and implement an urban agriculture pilot program. Service area: Papay and Port-au-Prince, Haiti.
- Haiti Hope House, Inc. Covers school fees and provides vocational for rural children. Service area: Mizak, Haiti.
- Haitian Artisans for Peace, International (HAPI). Project to offer growth, training, and technical support for staff and local community towards economic and gender equity. Service area: Mizak, Haiti.
- Chosen Ministry Haiti implements a Comprehensive Education Management Training project on healthcare and prevention of HIV/AIDS, malaria, cholera, and tuberculosis for women, children, and youth.

- Global Health Action. Building the opportunity for a livelihood and increased security to feed a family for mothers with malnourished children through training and establishment of a goat cooperative. Service area: Trouin, Haiti.

Jamaica

- United Theological College of the West Indies. Clinical pastoral education (CPE) and supervisor programs for faculty, students and clergy in Jamaica. CPE represents an internationally recognized standard of best practice for the training of ministers in pastoral care and counseling. Service area: Kingston, Jamaica.

Latin America and Caribbean

- CIEMAL. Support for the continental gathering of Methodist youth leaders throughout all Spanish speaking Methodist churches in Latin America and the Caribbean. Region wide.
- Christ Our Hope for Health and Abundant Hope. Partner: Latin America and Caribbean Region Methodist Women's Confederation. Service area: Event held in Santiago, Chile.

South Caribbean (St. Vincent and The Grenadines, St. Lucia, Barbados, Grenada, Trinidad and Tobago)

- Methodist Church of the Caribbean and Americas (MCCA) South Caribbean District is developing Children's Faith Development work to bring children into the Methodist Church by bridging gaps between children, their families, and the church, and by building, teaching, and encouraging faithful responses for parents, church staff, and students to respond to the issues facing children in the Caribbean today.

Uruguay

- Ministry with Women and the Elderly. Partner: Methodist Church in Uruguay. Program support to the Uruguay Methodist Women to implement and train leadership in domestic violence and reproductive health. Service area: Montevideo, Uruguay.

- Uruguay Methodist Church. The manufacturing of accessories to provide skills training and employment opportunity for youth with disabilities. Service area: Montevideo, Uruguay.

Higher Education Scholarships

Scholarships for higher education are granted to international students in Africa, Asia, Europe, Latin America, and the Caribbean. These proven leaders become clergy, community developers, medical professionals, etc. Scholarships awarded through this program are supported by the International Ministries fund, Project #3019240. Current scholarship recipients in Latin America come from Haiti, Colombia, Honduras, Ecuador, Nicaragua, and Peru.

Regional Missionary

Serna Samuel works with the leadership and membership of the Methodist Church in the Caribbean and Americas Women (MCCAW) organization and the wider church in the French- and English-speaking countries of the Caribbean and Americas. Service area: St. Vincent's and the Grenadines.

A missionary to Latin America is being appointed in 2015

Ubuntu Journeys

Ubuntu Journeys are unique, short-term mission service opportunities for United Methodist Women members to interact with the world through mission partners. Ubuntu Journeys are about women of faith coming together through shared mission to address social issues and discover new ways of working together, supporting one another, and growing spiritually. United Methodist Women Ubuntu participants will expand their understanding of issues that impact the world and their community through mutual learning with women from other cultures. Each Ubuntu Journey connects women to women for a faith and mission opportunity that will:

- Witness love and struggle; share challenges and opportunities.
- Enhance cultural awareness; exchange ideas and skills.
- Learn where the United Methodist Women's Mission giving goes to support programs in countries all over the world.
- Understand daily life with Methodist and United Methodist, grassroots and ecumenical sisters around the world.

Together with global sisters, United Methodist Women will share the human experience of worship, prayer, and spiritual reflection to engage in mission that will cultivate faith, hope, and love into action.

Upcoming Ubuntu Journeys to the following countries include:
Brazil
Chile
Costa Rica
Haiti
Uruguay

A woman in front of her home in Las Flores, Ixcan, Guatemala. *(Paul Jeffrey)*

A man mends a fishing net in a Honduran village along the Gulf of Fonseca. Along with other families in the village, he has lost access to some land and parts of the ocean in recent years as the wealthiest family in Honduras has moved in, fencing off vast areas. *(Paul Jeffrey)*

About the Author

Sonia Dias was born in São Paulo, Brazil, where she lives with her husband, Willem, and their two sons, Pedro, 19, and Ulisses, 15. She is a journalist with a master's degree in communications, and is currently a Ph.D. candidate in education at Universidade de São Paulo in Brazil. Sonia works at Editora FTD, a publishing house, with books and digital resources for education. She is a Humphrey Fellow with the Fulbright Program. During her internship at UNICEF in May of 2012 in New York, Sonia became associated with United Methodist Women and wrote the annotated bibliography for "Bearing Witness," an exhibit that took place during the Permanent Forum on Indigenous Issues at the Tillman Chapel in the Church Center for the United Nations.

Other Resources from United Methodist Women

Latin America: People and Faith in Spanish
By Sonia Maria Barbosa Dias
ISBN: 978-1-940182-17-9
M3224
$10

Latin America: People and Faith in Korean
By Sonia Maria Barbosa Dias
ISBN: 978-1-940182-18-6
M3225
$10

Latin America: People and Faith in Portuguese
By Sonia Maria Barbosa Dias
Kindle version
K3245
$5.35

response magazine, April 2015, focusing on Latin America

Place your order with:
United Methodist Women Mission Resources
1-800-305-9857
www.umwmissionresources.org

Latin America: People and Faith webpage:
www.unitedmethodistwomen.org/latinamerica

Kevin Rojas, aged 10, plays football at his home in Santa Victoria Este, Argentina. Rojas lives in an area of the Chaco where indigenous Wichí families, who traditionally survived as hunter-gatherers, have struggled against the systematic expropriation of their land for over a century by mestizo cattleraisers who migrated into the region from elsewhere in Argentina. In 2014, the two groups finally agreed on a division of the land which recognizes the traditional land rights of the indigenous, and which resettles many mestizo families—including that of Rojas—onto non-indigenous land. Church World Service has worked in partnership with local residents as they negotiated the landmark settlement. *(Paul Jeffrey)*

A Wichí indigenous boy climbs a tree in Santa Victoria Este, Argentina. *(Paul Jeffrey)*